FROM ENEMY TERRITORY

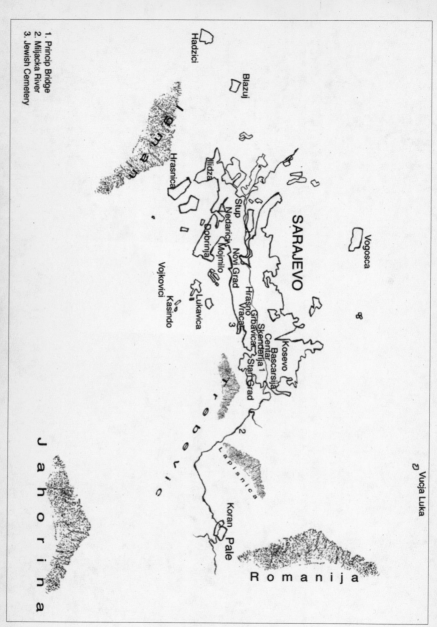

Map of Sarajevo and Environs

1. Princip Bridge
2. Miljacka River
3. Jewish Cemetery

Hadzici

Blazuj

Hrasnica

Ilidza

Stup

Nedarici

Dobrinja

Mojmilo

Novi Grad

Vojkovici

Kasindo

Lukavica

Vogosca

SARAJEVO

Hrasno

Grbavica

Vraca

Skenderija 1

Centar

Bascarsija

Stari Grad

Kosevo

Trebevic

Lapisnica

Koran

Pale

Romanija

Jahorina

Vucja Luka

Mladen Vuksanović

FROM ENEMY TERRITORY

Pale Diary
(5 April to 15 July 1992)

Foreword by
Joschka Fischer

SAQI
in association with
THE BOSNIAN INSTITUTE

British Library Cataloguing-in-Publication Data
A catalogue record for this book is available from the British Library

ISBN 0 86356 726 6
EAN 9 780863 567261

copyright © 2004 the estate of Mladen Vuksanović

translated for this edition by Quintin Hoare,
helped by an earlier version by Sonja Wild Bičanić
translation © 2004 The Bosnian Institute (London)

originally published as *Pale: dnevnik 5.4 – 15.7.1993*, Durieux (Zagreb) 1996
copyright © 1998 Durieux

foreword and afterword originally published in
Pale – im Herzen der Finsternis, Folio (Vienna) 1997
copyright © 1997 Folio

translated for this edition by Yasmine Gaspard
translation © 2004 Yasmine Gaspard

This edition first published 2004

SAQI
26 Westbourne Grove
London W2 5RH
www.saqibooks.com

in association with
The Bosnian Institute
14/16 St Mark's Road
London W11 1RQ
www.bosnia.org.uk

Contents

Glossary

B-H	Bosnia-Herzegovina
Baščaršija	old Ottoman bazaar in the centre of Sarajevo
čaršija	bazaar, urban quarter of merchants and craftsmen
Centre (*Centar*)	municipality in Sarajevo
chetnik	extreme Serb nationalist (see note 6 on page 29 below)
Children's Embassy (*Dječa ambasada*)	body set up by UNICEF to evacuate children from city
dimije	billowing trousers of traditional Turkish dress still worn by some rural women
Dobrotvor (benefactor)	charitable association
GRAS (*Gradski Saobračaj*)	urban public transport company
gusle	traditional Serb fiddle
Hidrogradnja	hydraulic engineering firm
INA	Croatian petrol company
JNA (*Jugoslavenska narodna armija*)	Yugoslav People's Army – army of the former Yugoslavia

7

Glossary

Kurban Bajram	Second most important Bosnian Muslim religious festival, marking the culmination of the annual pilgrimage to Mecca
Lower Town (*Donja čaršija*)	part of Pale
lozovača	grape brandy
MUP (*Ministarstvo unutarnih poslova*)	ministry of internal affairs, with its own police force
New Town (*Novi grad*)	municipality in Sarajevo
Obala	Embankment of the river Miljacka in Sarajevo
Old Town (*Stari grad*)	municipality in Sarajevo
PBS	*Privredna banka Sarajeva*
RTS	Radio Television Sarajevo
RTV	Radio and Television
SAO (*Srpska autonomna oblast*)	Serb Autonomous Region (see note 3 on page 22 below)
SDS (*Srpska demokratska stranka*)	Serb Democratic Party – Serb nationalist party led by Radovan Karadžić
SRNA (*Srpska republička novinska agencija*)	Serb Republic News Agency
Šipad	major pre-war firm exporting timber products
šljivovica	plum brandy
Šoping	tower block with ground level mall in Grbavica
TVS	TV Sarajevo
UNIS	firm giving name to prominent Sarajevo twin skyscrapers
Upper Town (*Gornja čaršija*)	part of Pale
ustasha	extreme Croat nationalist (see note 7 on page 48 below)

It Began in April

Foreword by
Joschka Fischer

'I cannot think, I cannot write, I cannot live.'
Pale, Monday 1 June 1992

When Viktor Klemperer's diaries were published in November 1995, they justifiably caused a great stir among the German reading public, with their depiction of a German Jew's life in Dresden during the years of National Socialism and with the author's views on the persecution of the Jews, the war and the Holocaust. Even though the events of National Socialism in Germany and the Nazi crimes against the European Jews are historically unique and therefore not replicable, much in the – well, what: Serb? Croat? Yugoslav? – journalist Mladen Vuksanović's record is reminiscent of Klemperer's diaries between 1933 and 1945. Vuksanović's memoirs were written in similar circumstances and deal with similar themes: namely the experience of – and survival from – eruptions of fascism, discrimination, exclusion and deportation, and the onset of death and war in the daily routines of ordinary people. This diary, however, does not recount former times, but inhabits a recent past – or a continuing present. Mladen Vuksanović writes about the rebirth of fascism in the nineties, not the thirties. This is what renders his account so deeply shocking, yet at the same time so extremely important. On 9 May 1992, a month after the outbreak of war and massacre in Bosnia, the author notes in his diary: 'Today is Victory over Fascism Day. In Europe and the rest of the world, but not here. Here fascism is being reborn and taking its toll of blood. The Balkans seem to me like an accursed fragment of the earth's crust where day occasionally dawns only for night to fall again.' The greater part of the German left unfortunately failed to acknowledge this rebirth of fascism in Europe. A look into Mladen Vuksanović's diary makes the extent of this failure very clear, so that it is not just instructive but hopefully beneficial for the future.

Mladen Vuksanović is a journalist and an intellectual with a critical spirit, who lived in Pale at the start of the 1992 Bosnian war.[1] His father was a Montenegrin and lies buried in the Orthodox cemetery; his mother, of Croato-Slovene origin, lies in the Catholic graveyard. The dead have their cemeteries, but where do the living belong? Those children of Yugoslav families who suddenly grew suspicious of one another, where do they belong? Thus we find ourselves at the very heart of this book, and also at the heart of Bosnia's insane, atrocious, bloody history. One of the more distressing features of this grim diary is its convincingly tranquil descriptions of the visits to the cemetery that eventually led to political suspicion and real danger in Pale. 'My weekly visit to my mother's grave suddenly becomes something odd, abnormal. They watch me with suspicion and mistrust. The stonemason who did the final work on her grave last year asks me why *obitelj* [Croatian word for 'family'] is used on the tombstone rather than *porodica*, why my mother is buried here and not next to my father in the Orthodox graveyard, and why I visit the graveyard every week when nobody else does so. He questions

---

1. Mladen Vuksanović died in 1999 on the island of Cres (Croatia), where his family had taken refuge and he worked at a children's home as careworker and night watchman, three years after Fischer wrote this foreword for the German edition of his Pale diary and a year before the posthumous publication of his novel *Taksi za Jahorinu* in Zagreb.

me as though he has the right, as a "pure-blooded Serb", to ask anything he wants.' This entry is from 3 May 1992.

Vuksanović is not politically active: he relies only on judgement and moral decency. He never allows the smallest shadow of doubt to arise about where the guilt lies for the unspeakable suffering that the war brought to the people of Bosnia: with Serb nationalism and its desire for a Greater Serbia. Milošević, Mladić, Karadžić are the names of those responsible, whom he by no means ignores in the course of his diary. Vuksanović, the maker of a television documentary about the destruction of Dubrovnik, is a very astute observer; but even he failed to grasp the extent to which the Serb soldateska's brutality and cold-blooded desire to slaughter was to descend upon Sarajevo and the Bosnian Muslims. The reality of everyday life in Europe, which helped determine the normal daily routine in Bosnia in 1992, did not allow for instantaneous recognition of the dangers associated with such an outburst of fascism. 'Our daughter, who went into town yesterday for some rock concert, phones from a girl friend's to say she will be home as soon as the barricades are lifted,' notes Vuksanović in his first diary entry on 5 April 1992. The daughter, a rock concert in Sarajevo and the start of a bloodbath – that is how mundanely the tremendous slaughter befell the citizens of Bosnia in that spring of 1992.

The author often quotes Franz Kafka, master of the absurd, and indeed the diary describes divided people, divided realities and divided cemeteries in war-shattered Bosnia: 'Two worlds (once one) only fifteen km. apart; one dies, suffers, weeps, the other shoots, plays music and sings,' is written on 2 May, as Serb shells strike Sarajevo. And Vuksanović writes about the daily enforcement of fascism: above all through the distinction between 'us' and 'them', between Serbs on the one hand and Croats and Muslims on the other. Vuksanović meticulously portrays the beginning of ostracism of 'them', followed by removal of their rights – the mark of all fascism.

'Another shock for Muslims in Pale. They have been fired from all state-owned enterprises and offices. One more step towards pure applied fascism... Step by step the new authorities in Pale are putting into practice Hitler's idea about the supremacy of one nation over another, about Aryans and Jews. Except it took Hitler a few years to do what these people have done in a few months,' reads the entry for 27 May 1992. And on 28 May: 'All Muslims have had their telephones cut off, they are forbidden to gather in "public places"... Muslims have been advised (for now) to leave Pale in the interest of their own safety. Nobody is driving them out, but...' Serb fascism was marching in accordance with historically proven models, and needed to advance blow by blow. Vuksanović writes about the growing terror aimed at Pale's Muslim community, escalating with the aim of forcing it to leave. He describes the panicked flight from pogroms occurring after severe Serb losses in the siege of Sarajevo; the clinging on to homes and farms, often the fruits of a lifetime's work; and finally the escape, saving nothing but their skins. It was to be no different for the author and his family. 'I look through some old newspapers (no papers at all arrive in Pale),' he notes on 20 May, 'and spot an old photograph of Hitler. He looks at me as though he had risen from his grave and was walking round me. He does not need to rise from the dead, his successors are already all about me.'

And with fascism come also new masters, the loss of friends to the blood-filled insanity, and the cruelty and corruption of most of its supporters: 'He was a child of communism,' reads the entry for 10 May about a lawyer, once a family friend, 'now he's a child of the blackest nationalism. This is a time that exposes people totally, their make-up is off and the lies show a person's true face. And that face frightens me.' Time and again you encounter succinct statements evoking chronicles of horror: 'In Sarajevo there is a shortage of wood for coffins.' (24 May) 'They are still bombarding Sarajevo. The Holiday Inn, the railway station, the UNIS building... The people from the hills must be direct descendants of Nero.' (25 May)

Mladen Vuksanović devotes almost a special chapter to settling scores with his own profession of journalism. Colleagues and friends from yesterday have turned into the deadly enemies of today, and nobody can explain why. Ideological madness, careerism, corruption and fear supersede for many colleagues the illuminatory aspiration of independent journalism. Vuksanović's disgust at such depravity in his own profession is obvious from the following notes: 'Horror upon horror. In the centre of the city, in Vaso Miskin street next to the Market, a shell falls on people queuing for bread. Scores dead and hundreds wounded ... On Serb TV from Pale, my former colleague Rada Đokić says that the Muslims themselves have done this deliberately, the "green berets" that is, in order to shock the world. I'm beginning to hate my profession from the bottom of my heart. They're not journalists, they're professional killers.' (27 May.)

Mladen Vuksanović's diary is a subtle book about the early stages of the decimation of the Bosnian Muslims, and for that reason it leaves an even more intense impression. He has not witnessed the mass shootings, the barbaric torture, the mass rapes or the concentration camps, so has little to report about these atrocities. This somehow renders all the more powerful his depiction of the changes in everyday social life on the Bosnian Serb side, which first made those war crimes possible. Fear for your children's lives; creeping anxiety for your own survival; yearning for flight, for a safer refuge, for escape from the nationalistic madness; the necessity of desertion for young men of fighting age, threatened with conscription to an assured death sentence – we (and above all our interior minister) should read this diary diligently, before Germany too hastily sends back the Bosnian refugees, seen by many as useless scroungers, to an unknown fate.

One final observation: 'Justice for Serbs' is how Peter Handke's unspeakable text attempting to justify Greater Serbian nationalism is subtitled. That justice is presently being fought for on the streets of Belgrade by students and the democratic opposition. We can also find justice in the diary of Mladen Vuksanović, who does not differentiate between Serbs and Muslims, but – mercilessly – between the guilty and the innocent, between criminals and victims. 'The Serbs do not deserve to be led by a banker and a psychiatrist [Milošević and Karadžić] down the road to crime and destruction', he notes on 11 June 1992. Had anyone found these records, whether in his house in Pale or on his escape-route, it would certainly have meant his death sentence. Precisely because he does not get involved in the fanaticism of bloodthirsty nationalism, unlike a Handke only pretending to avoid politics, Mladen Vuksanović creates that 'justice for Serbs' which has degenerated to mere propaganda in Handke's case. Moreover, because a non-military, European and democratic Serbia needs such justice for a future beyond bloodshed and nationalism – it is good that Mladen Vuksanović's diary is henceforth available also in translation. It should at least compel the left to scrutinize its conscience with regard to its own failure.

February 1997

Author's Preface

In Pale, where I was born and had lived since 1984, I spent 110 (one hundred and ten) days in a peculiar isolation because, as an editor and writer for TV Sarajevo, I refused to work for the Serb television in Pale. A 'complicating' factor was also my late mother's Croat-Catholic background (she was buried in the Catholic graveyard, rather than beside my father in the Orthodox one), as well as the fact that both my daughter and my son were born in Rijeka (Croatia), where my wife's family lives.

This diary was written under permanent stress, in the fear that it would be found if my house was searched; then, hidden in my luggage as I passed eight security checks on my journey from Pale to the Hungarian border, it was brought to Rijeka.

In it, I recorded only what I personally saw, heard, or felt on my own skin. Because of my inability to move around freely, I was not able to witness or to register many events that took place in Pale. But I am sure that others who survived torture on the 'free territory of the Serb Republic of Bosnia-Herzegovina' will testify about these one day.

I have expanded the original diary only by such additions as will make it easier for a reader to understand my notes.

I know that publishing this diary will earn me their death sentence; but I also know that not to publish it because of that would mean to die of shame for my silence.

In writing this diary I have had the selfless support of my wife Jadranka, who in my worst moments encouraged me to carry on to the end.

Pale Diary

5 April to 16 May 1992

Pale, Sunday 5 April 1992

Barricades again in Sarajevo! Sealed up in Pale like a bird in a cage, I'm reminded of one of Kafka's dreadful sentences: 'A cage went in search of a bird'.

The shock is terrible. There is no one on the main street, it's deserted. My wife, quixotically, in a show of protest and solidarity with the Sarajevans, puts our dog Žuža on a lead and goes out for a walk with our neighbour Mina in order to show how 'man is free'. People have withdrawn into their houses to listen to Radio Sarajevo broadcasting all that's going on in the city.

Our daughter, who went into town yesterday for some rock concert, phones from a girl friend's to say she'll be home as soon as the barricades are lifted.

I walk out onto the street and see armed men in the distance, milling around the police station. I console myself that tomorrow will bring peace, that everything is just an ugly, fearful dream. With that hope I go to bed.

Pale, Monday 6 April 1992

The day of Sarajevo's liberation from Fascism, forty-seven years ago. Today it's a city seeking to liberate itself anew.

My daughter and son are there. I sent my son to Sarajevo a month ago, to save him from being called up here in Pale.

My wife calls the police to ask how she'll get to work tomorrow. The duty officer gives her a short answer: 'You won't, the Lapišnica tunnel is mined.'

I ask myself whether that's possible and what it means? How can they just 'cut us off' from the city like that? My mind is a nightmare of a thousand questions for which I have no rational answer. Loathing, I feel nothing but loathing for this people.

On Sarajevo TV I watch a young woman from Dubrovnik, who had come to Sarajevo to study, killed at the barricades near the Vrbanja bridge. God, can this be true?

In the evening, Pale looks like a tomb waiting for the dead. In Sarajevo, instead of celebrating Liberation Day they're counting the dead and the wounded.

My wife spends the whole night watching TV.

Pale, Tuesday 7 April 1992

There are two books on my bedside table: Gunter Anders's *Kafka, For and Against*, in a brilliant translation by Ivan Foht whose lectures on aesthetics I attended at university; and *Jesus Christ* Part I by Rudolf Wiener, in an edition dating from 1932. I cannot believe that Jesus said: 'He who is not for me is against me.' I don't know any ideology that has not woven this principle into its programme.

I quite believe one of Kafka's sentences, which goes more or less like this: 'I was sitting at an inn, when two uniformed men burst in and ordered me to go with them. "But I'm a civilian", I told them, "I'm a free man." "That's just why", they said and took me away.'

I phone in 'live' to a Radio Sarajevo programme to say that no one can get out of Pale (just 16 km away from Sarajevo), and that JNA soldiers and local Serb forces are in control of all major and minor roads leading to the city.

Last night my wife and I went to see some old friends of ours, who had been witnesses at our wedding. Their son, a doctor who works in Sarajevo, only just made it through the barricades on Sunday; they barely let him return home to Pale. But next morning an army vehicle came for him, and now he has to work at the newly established military hospital. We can't believe it: the hotel in Koran transformed into a fully equipped military hospital.

How naive and blind I am! So wrapped up in my work – writing a story called 'Taxi to Jahorina', on the basis of which by 1 May 1992 I have to hand in to Forum Movies the script for a feature film – that I can't see anything around me.[2] Or I do see, but so little and just trivia.

On TV I look at smashed and looted shops in Sarajevo. In Pale they're not smashed, but they're totally empty. I remember the time after the War (1950), when the only shop in Pale had nothing but chicory (ersatz coffee), so we used to call the shopkeeper 'Chicory' and he'd chase us out with his stick. Only

2. The work was transformed into a novel once the author reached his place of refuge on the island of Cres, and was published posthumously as *Taksi za Jahorinu* in 2000.

last year at this time I could still walk freely at night in the woods round Pale, thinking about my 'Taxi-driver'. A month ago I stopped walking through the woods even by day, as it had become too dangerous. Four days ago in the evening I was walking along the road past the graveyard when an armed guy suddenly appeared out of the darkness. He couldn't understand how anyone could still be walking around like that after dark. He asked me for my surname, and when I told him he advised me: 'Be careful, because they (the Muslims) are here in the woods.'

Pale, Wednesday 8 April 1992

The Pale people are shelling Sarajevo, the Old Town and my friends who live there!

The sound of a phone in the empty house (the children are in Sarajevo, friends can't come because of the barricades and the shooting, while everyone I know in Pale is glued to the TV watching what's happening 'down there').

It's a friend of mine, a colleague (V.) from TV Sarajevo, calling to ask me: 'How can they fire so indiscriminately from Trebević and Lapišnica?'

I can't understand his question. Should they perhaps first come into the city and stick a label on certain houses, families or individuals?

But why are they bombarding the city in the first place? What do they hope to achieve with that? It's crazy, I say to myself.

A colleague of mine (V.T.) from RTV calls me. I'd never have dreamed she could leave the city and her old mother, and settle in at Hotel Bistrica on Jahorina. Her newest friend, a doctor and politician, once a fierce Communist and then a Reformist, is now a fierce Serb. The colleague asks me when I'm going to start working for their 'Serb Television News Centre'. I'm disturbed and a bit scared. She doesn't ask 'whether' I will, but 'when', as if it were a foregone conclusion. She tells me the names of other colleagues who have already transferred to Pale and are starting to work here. First I say that I was never a political journalist, and that I now have a job to do for the UN High Commission for Refugees; then finally, when I gather my thoughts a bit, I manage to come up with a phrase that I have uttered many times before, about how: 'I'm not a national, but a professional journalist.' There's a long silence at the other end of the line, then the voice that a moment ago had been so gentle and pleasant grows shrill and says that I should 'think carefully about what I'm doing'.

I know what that means, which is why I'm afraid.

The telephone rings again and I hear the faraway voice of a dear one, full of fear and anxiety for us. Perhaps we really should all have left before this Balkan feast.

Going is the easiest part, but how am I to leave this house which I've built over the years with my own hands and cultivated the garden round it?

Today I dig the garden a bit and plant some currant bushes. I hope I'll taste their fruit.

The horror of the television, all the fear and the shooting. It's night and it's raining. Everything is dark, a real scene from my 'Taxi-driver' story. I MUST go on writing it, but how, when I'm listening intently and with trepidation for the brusque footsteps of people coming to take me away?

I think constantly about my son and my daughter, cut off in Sarajevo. Neither they nor I can any longer pass the frontier they established a few days ago on Lapišnica. It's as though some powerful, ruthless hand has cut us in two, with or without the hope that we'll join up again. God, is this possible?

22.00

Now my wife, who is watching TV, calls out that some officials of SAO Romanija i Jarčedol-Hreša are negotiating, and will decide whether or not to 'open the frontier'.[3] Do they even know how to negotiate? I picture Neanderthals building computers.

What will this night be like? The only certainty is that dawn will come.

V., a friend from Sarajevo, tells me over the phone that it's easier for me in my graveyard than for him in town listening to shells exploding. He is mistaken.

I go to bed and dream about Istria as a dream realized.

I never knew that the darkness here was so dark.

I am beginning – wrongly I know – to hate the very word 'nation'. A nation isn't to blame because in its bosom it feeds and nourishes monsters. Only three years ago, on the island of Krk, a close friend kept insisting that I should say what I was, which nation I belonged to. She looked at me in disbelief when I said that I was just a human being and nothing more. For her, a human being without national identity simply does not exist.

The curtains are drawn on the windows of all the neighbouring houses.

---

3.   The SDS led by Radovan Karadžić began to establish para-state structures called 'Serb Autonomous Provinces' (SAO) from September 1991, following a model already tested in Croatia, in preparation for the assault on B-H that was launched in April 1992.

How absurd it is. Two months ago in Dubrovnik I was filming a short documentary about the destruction of the city, called 'The Devil Unleashed', when a man told me I didn't need to film them because I'd soon be experiencing on my own skin, in Sarajevo and in Bosnia, the horrors they were now going through. I didn't believe him, I didn't want to believe him.

Pale, Thursday 9 April 1992

A sleepless night. With the aid of *Signs by the Roadside* I try to decipher the future course of our madness.[4] I feel as though a kind of metastasis is spreading around me, swelling and expanding just like the bread dough I knead with my own hands every morning.

I look at my wife, who is happily picking rocket in the garden, and I think about that 'political type' from Serbia who threatened last year that we'd soon be eating roots.

I keep in touch every day by phone with the cameramen A.V. and A.S. and give them instructions on how to film a Sarajevo version of 'The Devil Unleashed'.

My neighbour Meho comes to see me in a state of terror, saying that there's a rumour going round Pale that tonight 'all Muslims will be slaughtered'.

I convince him that this is impossible. He and his wife should sleep at our place tonight. I look at his hands, trembling with fear. I understand that fear, because I too feel it in my bones: fear that I shan't see the next day dawn.

---

4.   *Znakovi pored puta*: volume of reflections noted down throughout his life by Nobel-Prize-winning Bosnian writer Ivo Andrić.

I think about an acquaintance of mine from TV Sarajevo, a producer called M.T., who is now starting up the Serb TV News Centre in Pale. 'At last our side of the story will be heard.'

Is he doing it out of conviction, out of fanaticism, or for money? While he was working for TV Sarajevo, he did what he wanted, nobody ever banned him from doing anything, and now he fumes about having been 'discriminated against and handicapped'. I told him even then that only the stupid and the lazy were handicapped, but I don't think it sank in.

The new Serb authorities pay them like the most expensive whores. I refused to work for them as 'TV Sarajevo's most respected documentary film-maker', so now I'm awaiting my sentence. I wonder if they can even understand my statement that I'm not a national journalist but a professional one, and that the two are incompatible.

I dredge up from my memory Kafka's sentence from *The Castle*: 'Mr K., you're not from the Castle, you're not from the village, you aren't anything.'

I watch a man in Pale's empty supermarket. He takes a tin and puts it in his basket, then returns it to the shelf, then puts it in his basket again and once more returns it. In the end he just grabs some old biscuits. He surveys the empty shelves with unbelievable fury.

In the evening I watch the Belgrade TV news and am convinced yet again that some reporters are murderers and war criminals, worse even than the people who are destroying Sarajevo and killing civilians from the surrounding hills. For deranged and blinded minds, their words are the only signpost.

I watch TV Sarajevo and see one leader (Karadžić) rejecting any possibility that the members of 'his people' can be called citizens, another leader (Izetbegović) claiming that all members of 'his people' are citizens, while the third (Kljujić) observes from the wings and announces smugly that 'his people' is first and foremost a European nation.

I ask myself: who am I then?

Pale, 10 April 1992

Early morning. My friend M.J. calls from TV Sarajevo to say that: 'It's been like thunder over the city all night long.' I can't believe it, I don't want to believe that a replay of Dubrovnik can happen in Sarajevo. Two cities with similar people and known across the world.

The wife of a TV cameraman, in tears, tells me what a mistake she made by not escaping with her children before the horror began.

On this precise day in 1945 Radio Sarajevo started broadcasting. When we celebrated it in past years, we gave out awards for good work, went to bars, and kissed one another. Happy days. Will they ever return?

Wrote one paragraph of 'Taxi to Jahorina':
The Count's serious face breaks into a happy, boyish grin, he stretches his arms wide and looks at the sky covered with dark clouds from which snow is beginning to fall.
"Yes, I am his child", he shouts with a thunderous laugh. It was not the normal laugh of a happy man. More like an avalanche plunging down a snowy cliff to rise once more to dizzy heights, rebound off a rock face and with new force like an echo dissipate among rocky peaks and sail above a gentle, sleepy valley.

It was the kind of laugh that scatters and drives away every fear, that instils hope that all is not yet lost, a ray of light breaking like a sword through the black, clinging mass of the darkness.'

They tell me in a shop that they no longer accept PBS cheques. And what does that mean? I'll soon find out, but it will probably be too late to do anything with those useless pieces of paper.

What does 'capturing Pale' mean to me and mine? Or the partition of B-H into private feuds controlled by crazy individuals? My children in one country, my wife and I in another, without any possibility of crossing that border, the frontier of death, our own Berlin Wall.

11.00

It begins to snow rather hard. Will it 'cool down the hot-heads', as my mother used to say?

One of the characters from my 'Taxi-driver' is called Čitavo [All], because when he was young his mother always used to ask him whether he wanted her to fry him a whole egg or just half. Earlier on I thought about frying two eggs for lunch myself, but I changed my mind at the last minute and fried only one. I smile. Before you know it the distant past comes back as present reality, relentless and terrible.

I stroke my dog Žuža and wonder how I'm ever going to feed her. Stale bread and a bit of lard, I tell myself, and hope she's not in pup.

My wife went for a walk around Pale. She came back shocked by the amount of cars without number plates. It's the more brazen of them driving stolen cars, vans or trucks without any shame.

But there was a comic touch about it even so: one car with no numbers simply had 'ACO' written on the plate – in Latin script![5]

Also, an unusual number of trucks loaded with timber. Serbian plates. Leaving Pale, obviously headed for 'the Motherland'.

Nightmare. Some man (Murat Šabanović) wants to blow up the Višegrad hydro-electric plant. That would be a total cataclysm.

Pale, 11 April 1992

What day is it today? A week has just gone by in a second, in an ugly terrible second. As time becomes more condensed, days turn into hours, hours into minutes and minutes seconds. Isolated and totally cut off from Sarajevo, we float like fish on the surface of polluted water, awaiting a swift end.

An entirely sleepless night. A gravel path leads to my house. Every step taken upon it echoes like the judge's gavel in a courtroom. It thrusts into my brain, causing some 'slight unease'. Are those the footsteps of executioners coming to get us?

Fear has sneaked into everyone and gnaws at them like a cancer. I sense death breathing all about me.

Yesterday my wife had a little attack of nerves because of our being totally sealed off in Pale, without any hope of seeing our children and friends in the city. She began writing a letter to the Pale council chairman, R. Starčević, a young man who three years ago helped his father fix ceramic tiles in our bathroom. As she writes the letter in a frenzy of emotion, I say to her:
'If you send it off, we're done for, they'll come here and kill us. If you're ready for that, then send it off.'

---

5.   Aco is a typically Serbian shortening of the name Alexander.

She calms down and stops writing, and I stow the letter away in our secret archive.

Here is a copy of that letter:

> *Comrade Starčević,*
>
> *I recently heard you on the Sarajevo TV evening news programme, when you called in to deny a report that people from Sarajevo were maltreated if they went up Mt Jahorina. You ended by saying that Pale had always been a hospitable tourist centre, and you even invited people from Sarajevo to come and see for themselves.*
>
> *I do not know if you remember me. My husband and I own that house in Pale to the construction of which your own hands made a contribution, and especially those of your father, who spoke so interestingly about life in Sweden. About their big windows and spacious bathrooms. Do you remember us and our bathroom now?*
>
> *At the time, when my friends from the city asked me why we were building a house in Pale, I used to reply that we wanted to live in the European way: work in the city and then spend the rest of the day out in the country, in the peace of what was once a health resort.*
>
> *I do not know how many days it has been now that I have no peace, cannot go to the city to work, cannot go anywhere. I do not know how many days it has been that they have been shelling Sarajevo from Lapišnica. I hear that people from Pale are doing this, and that Jahorina too is full of soldiers. I do not know how many days it has been now that I have been watching TV news bulletins full of horrors, while I still have not heard you denying THAT. Is it really possible that you are unaware of the fact that people from Pale are destroying the city in which you too were a student?! Is it really possible that you, as a civil engineer, are quite unaffected by the sight of that destruction?! Is it really possible that you know all this, but have sold yourself and your birthplace so cheaply? Is it possible that you do not have at least one friend to worry about in Sarajevo?'*

In the evening an acquaintance comes over, M.T., a producer from the Serb Radio and TV station that is about to start broadcasting in Pale. A long conversation with him destroys even the faintest hope for calm. I don't drink anything, he drinks cognac. With every sip his rage grows towards me and towards the 'Turks' who have to be wiped out. He takes a pistol from his belt and threatens me because I won't work for them. I tell him that I'm fifty years old, that I've seen enough, got drunk with my friends enough, loved enough beautiful women, so now if he wants to he can shoot. The only thing I regret is not finishing my novel/screenplay 'Taxi to Jahorina'. My wife is terrified by his looks, his speech and his pistol, so she goes off to her work room on the first floor.

M.T attacks me more and more aggressively for not being a true member of 'their people', not doing anything for it, being a traitor. I explain to him that I am pure and of clear conscience. (Can anyone have a clear conscience today? Haven't we all to some extent arranged the pieces of the mosaic of this darkness that is devouring us?)

M.T repeats that he is a 'true chetnik',[6] that thousands of 'Serb guards' – and Arkan's men too – are on Jahorina, merely waiting for the order before swooping down on Sarajevo. And he recounts how outside the supermarket he saw his own car, which had been stolen in Sarajevo a month ago, but didn't dare take it, since he knows that all manner of dregs who'll stop at nothing have come to Pale. And the whole time he is explaining to me sadistically how killing a man is a kind of sexual excitement.

6. Traditional term for irregular fighters, adopted in World War II by royalist forces under Draža Mihailović which collaborated with the Axis occupiers and carried out massacres of Muslims, then again in the 1990s by Serbian irregulars (e.g. those organized by Vuk Drašković, Vojislav Šešelj and Željko Ražnjatović Arkan) fighting in Croatia and Bosnia, where in response the term was widely used to describe all Serbs siding with the aggression organized from Belgrade.

A great deal of our conversation cannot be written down, since today words can kill more quickly than a bullet. If they find this diary of mine, they won't kill me but roast me on a spit.

Around midnight the director goes out into the impenetrable, sticky Pale darkness. In a cheap thriller that serves as toilet paper in the loo, I come across a passage by chance that in exactly the same words describes the sexual arousal of one of its characters, some criminal or murderer: '... Besides, killing has always held a unique attraction for Warren Felker. Blood on his own hands created the excitement within him that other people experience during an intense orgasm...'

And on the other side of the torn-off passage, only now do I notice this text: '... He believes that he is still the dictator of some wretched little state, and that I should stand still and tremble in front of him! Just wait until he hears our price...he'll soon change his tune!...'

This morning at the butcher's I got the last soup bone. Dogs too should be fed.

I tell the cameraman V. he should film the hungry, his reply: 'Well, I'm hungry!'

I run into an old Muslim lady on the street, she hugs me and says tearfully: 'God has taken everything that was valuable.'

At around noon, the panicky voice on the phone of our close friend B.O. from Sarajevo asks me how she can get out of the city, which is looking more and more like a rat-infested ruin.

We're worried and check with mutual friends what this was all about. They reassure us, saying that the O.s are far too emotional.

I think about Istria and Italy as our still unrealized dream. Are we going to survive this horror and realize our dream? I'll leave all this without pain or regret: the new house, the garden, the books we have been collecting for years. I know why. I still have enough energy, even though I'm fifty, to start from scratch. They can take my home, burn it, destroy it, but they cannot erase my memories of the days when I was building it.

Pale, 12 April 1992

'Viennese breakfast' – a slice of bread smeared with lard!

What a sad Sunday has dawned. Snow on the budding branches of the currant bushes in the garden. The first night without being periodically awoken from slumber. When he is exhausted, a man becomes indifferent to what will happen.

Is this the summit of the hill of death, now to be followed by relaxation and descent, or is there still a climb ahead?

We no longer have enough candles for the graves, so I'll cut one in half. On my mother's grave, green shoots are pushing irresistibly through last year's grass. I stand and say to myself: 'Thank you, God, for letting my mother die three years ago, without waiting for this horror.' She barely survived two world wars, never lost the fear that it might happen again. She died peaceful and happy, without pain or protracted suffering. Her last wish was to be buried in the Catholic graveyard, next to her ancestors. My father was buried in the Orthodox graveyard. They were like one being, a happy union of two faiths, two nations, mutual respect and love at whose fire I warmed myself.

My sister rings in a panic from Titograd, saying I should evacuate the children from Sarajevo on a military aircraft, 'because THEY will certainly raze the city to the ground'. I lose my temper and shout that if they're such monsters, let them destroy everything and kill everyone. The television shows apocalyptic scenes from the airport, where crowds of women, children and men are storming the planes. Francis Ford Coppola already shot all these scenes in 'Apocalypse Now'.

The EU's Cutileiro, together with local leaders, has divided up the TV into national channels. When all's said and done, maybe this is even a good thing. When they get nationalism out of their system, maybe the journalists will start working professionally.

There's no food in the shops, but plenty of expensive toilet paper.

My wife retreats to her work room and is weaving something on the loom.

In semi-darkness I listen to a CD, Mozart's 35th Symphony in D major. What does Mozart sound like in Pale? Mozart was a child of God.

Pale, Monday 13 April 1992

A beautiful spring morning with frost covering the garden. With an extreme effort I do my morning exercises. Is it because of my age or too little food?

A deafening explosion echoes over Pale. I find out that some military hero in a MIG has broken the sound barrier over Pale and Sarajevo. I picture him in his pilot's gear, and a mother in some miserable little room just nursing her baby.

On the road in front of the house, various people approach me and immediately start expounding their 'absolutely genuine' versions of the truth about what is happening around us. They talk endlessly like water-mills, hiding their fear. I listen to them like an idiot, nodding my head, then escape to my garden. I watch from my window as every so often some acquaintance of mine walks past in uniform, with a kalashnikov on his shoulder. Formerly as civilians insignificant and drab, they now hurry off heads high 'to report to their units'. As if for their whole lives they had just been waiting for this moment. One of them has already asked me if I have 'joined up'.

I notice that the bakery across the road, owned by some Albanians, is closed for the first time in fifteen years.

Pale, Tuesday 14 April 1992

The TV news programme is becoming the most popular horror-film here. Therein lies its power and magic. All the evil that has happened throughout the Republic that day is concentrated and condensed into 60 minutes and the half square metre of the screen. It has the effect on people of an explosion in a confined space. I think that a lot more people, especially the elderly, will die of television than of bullets.

We speak by telephone to our children. They have less and less food, and are finding it harder and harder to leave the house.

The hunger is only beginning. More and more helicopters arrive in Pale from the direction of Serbia and Montenegro. What can they be carrying, I wonder. 'Soldiers and arms', says our neighbour. Pale increasingly resembles a military camp, in which civilians have no place.

Last night on TV I listen to our renowned director Emir Kusturica, giving us from Paris his diagnosis of our sickness and his prescriptions for curing it. The populace at large has already got wise to him, though only yesterday he was their idol. How grotesque his words sound. As if he'd landed from Mars.

On Serb radio I listen to my colleagues of yesterday calling on 'their people' finally to settle its accounts with 'Islamic fundamentalists'. Only last year they were appealing to 'their communists' finally to settle accounts with all nationalists. Now they work for a different boss, who if he had any intelligence would know that he had sown the seeds of his future destruction. Jesus really was crucified in vain.

At two o'clock today negotiations between the board of TV Sarajevo and the SDS, at Hotel Srbija in Ilidža, about dividing up the TV channels. If they'd just stop killing people, they can divide up the sun, the moon, the air, the birds, the fish and anything else that's indivisible.

My wife talks on the phone to our best friend in Sarajevo J.O., who tells her he could strangle with his bare hands another friend of ours, the poet I.K., because he didn't like his comments made on a TV news programme. Just three months ago they were sitting round at our place, drinking and chatting.

22.30

The last lights have gone out in the neighbouring houses.

Pale, Wednesday 15 April 1992

Spring, real spring has arrived in Pale.

'A lovely day. Pity it's the last one.' – The words of my friend M.J

I start digging in our garden and plant some carrots. I've always loved this time of year best, when everything is awakening, and I tell myself on waking: 'Thank God I'm alive!'.

One of our neighbours, a Muslim lady (I used never to pay any attention to this before), says that because of 'the situation' she can't do a thing, but that when she sees me she at once feels better. It's mainly Muslims living round my house, we've always helped and respected each other. Now I can see – sense in fact – how frightened they are of what is to come. They go down less and less to the Lower Town, since that's where the police, the military and the television are based. Gathered on the nearby bridge, they watch in fear as a long column of military trucks goes by, with men in uniform peering out through the canvas hoods. Their neighbours of yesterday walk around with submachine-guns, don't greet them, and behave like a superior human breed.

I realize how blind I have been:

The new Serb authorities have taken over all the hotels in Pale and on Jahorina for their personal use. Villas and the more commodious weekend cottages, predominantly owned by Sarajevo Muslims, have been seized, and junior or senior officials of the new regime have moved into them. The hotel in Koran has been turned into a military hospital, staffed by Serb doctors who left Sarajevo in advance and transferred to Pale. The football field has become a strictly guarded helicopter landing field. The old cinema where I saw my first films has become a prison for Muslims and disobedient Serbs. The Cultural Centre (and Centre for War Victims!) has been converted for the needs of the new Serb TV and information centre. The flag of the Serb Democratic Party flutters over the police station, while the entire civil administration in the municipality is now subordinate to the new authorities. Everywhere in Pale and on the surrounding hills checkpoints have been set up, in order to control the movement of civilians. Hotel Panorama, owned by 'Hidrogradnja' from Sarajevo, has become the main seat of the new authorities. The INA petrol station was confiscated from its owner even earlier; and so on.

It's night, full moon. I have a deep feeling of unease, because of the coming rain and the new, unfamiliar people who are taking over Pale.

Pale, Thursday 16 April 1992

A sad, rainy spring morning again, more like autumn. How quickly a person adapts to everything. Accepts the abnormal as normal, accepts an impossible life as the only possible kind. Bare survival acquires its full meaning.

Nettles have begun to grow in our garden. Along with rocket, a new pleasure for my wife. And a new food.

The richer Muslims are exchanging their houses in Pale with Serbs from Sarajevo's Old Town. You sign a document with no legal authority at the municipality, you pack your most essential and most valuable belongings, you pay 'the appropriate people' a few hundred DM for safe passage on side roads to Sarajevo, and everything is settled within a day. I've also heard comments from 'ordinary Muslims', who say that only people who got rich quick under communism are now running away, fearing the vengeance of the 'clients' they cheated. But their own fear has increased even more, since they know that: 'if those prominent, rich people are running away, they surely know better than us ordinary folk what's in store.'

This is how five hundred years of common life are melting away, and new national ghettos being created.

I keep telling myself: 'Get as far away from all this as possible.'

Yet I feel disgust for the people behaving like rats on a sinking ship.

My phone has started 'singing'. I speak to my friend V.J. from Sarajevo, and he tells me to turn down the music in the house: really, how can I even listen to music while people in Sarajevo are dying?

I try to explain that they've connected up my telephone to the Serb radio programme from Pale, so that now all day long whenever I lift the receiver I hear either the news or their music. It's beginning to drive me out of my mind. I think about Orwell and his 1984: only now, when I'm experiencing it on my own skin, do I understand 'what the writer really meant'.

I pick up the phone and hear the line of a song: 'I pay my debts/ I must return them'.

Relief when our children call, or those wonderful people who have taken them in. Then we know that it's calm in Sarajevo and they're in the flat. When the phone keeps ringing and nobody answers, terror floods over us.

Pale, 17 April 1992

Today is (Catholic) Good Friday, a day when in our house we've never eaten meat, only fish. Luckily, we've saved a tin of sardines.

Fuel has arrived at the petrol station. An enormous queue of 'poor and oppressed' people is waiting to fill up their tanks. Everyone says they've nothing to eat, yet they're paying astronomic prices for the fuel. This country, this people, is made of deceit and cheap, transparent lies. Its language is essentially untrue. At times I want to howl with rage because I was born here and live here.

From my telephone receiver I hear the eleven o'clock news, about how after a trial run the Serb radio station in Pale has begun to broadcast programmes throughout the day. Such a fuss about something that's basically trivial. The Serbs have conquered this area physically, so of course they'll now try to conquer the hearts and minds of their own people. It's what the communists did too. Stuff people with only your own truths, turn them into robots who 'love what they are supposed to love'. O God, can we ever hope to rid this land of fascism?

On the Serb radio, jolly, optimistic, triumphal music, more necessary to the people than food. Radio Sarajevo is broadcasting quiet, sentimental music. All just fifteen kilometres apart.

First the army and the Serbs fought a war in Slovenia (I made a documentary about it), then they moved on to Croatia (I made a documentary about that), and now they've arrived in Bosnia-Herzegovina. I predict that after this Sandžak and Kosova will inevitably follow. This is the Balkan recipe for conquering territory and creating a national state. Everyone conquers territory, no one souls.

This telephone will drive me crazy. I yell into the receiver like a madman and for the umpteenth time try to explain that the music is not playing in my house.

Pale, Saturday 18 April 1992

The morning isn't rainy like autumn, but snowy like winter. Ten centimetres of snow as if heralding a long, cold winter. As if it were Christmas tomorrow, not Easter.

Scenes from my childhood keep coming to me, when for both Catholic and Orthodox Easter I'd be bathed and nicely dressed, in clean clothes. 'Childhood was a dream', the painter Paul Klee says somewhere.

A desperate, sad day – within me and all round me. Sarajevo was bombed again – GRAS, the Children's Embassy, UNIS, the Railway clinic, the area round TV Sarajevo.

When I walked round the ruined parts of Dubrovnik, I kept asking myself why they'd done it, what they'd wanted to show or prove, whether they weren't just destructive by nature. 'Father, forgive them, for they know not what they do!', says Jesus. I cannot understand those words.

Pale, Sunday 19 April 1992

Easter – in some ways my favourite day in the year. Because of the springtime burgeoning within me and all round me. The new energy, strength and will growing within me, as if foretelling a long life to come. Or is that only an illusion?

Visit to my mother's grave, where I light half a candle. After that I visit my father's grave (on the other side of Pale) and light the other half. I think of all the horrors they must have been through during the last war. They were a synthesis of two religions and two nations, and I carry this link within myself like something indestructible. They were quiet, unobtrusive believers of the kind God loves most, and they passed this love on to me. When my father killed himself in 1962 because his land had been nationalized, my mother didn't begin to hate the communists, she just kept repeating: 'God sees all and punishes all.'

For people today, religion and nation are just useful concepts that they'll throw away like used tissues when they don't need them anymore. In the name of their own interests they destroy what is indestructible.

On my way back from the graveyard, I watch a young man in uniform at one of the checkpoints that have sprung up all over

Pale, holding the barrel of his kalashnikov against his cheek and stroking it gently with one hand in a way that resembles pure masturbation.

In the yard of a house near the road another young man (I know his father, an honest man) is using an electric drill to remove the big GRAS (urban transport) signs from a stolen minibus. Honest fathers and criminal sons. Or everything has dissolved into a hopeless collapse of all human values.

The now familiar deafening noise of an army helicopter over the house tells me clearly where I am and who I am.

The snow in the garden is melting. Will this madness melt as quickly I wonder? It will, it has to, but not soon. Perhaps in five years. Lebanon lasted more than fifteen years, and this is worse than Lebanon.

My daughter sighs when we tell her we've saved some coloured eggs for her and her brother. She asks if there's milk in Pale. Just milk and eggs, nettles and rocket, we reply. She says those are the first things to sell out in the market, and the shops are nearly empty.

Pale, Monday, 20 April 1992

I begin to count off our third week in isolation. It's strange how a person gets used to this state, and remains silent, curses, or talks endlessly.

My wife tells me she saw some people in civilian clothes at the bank, in the crowd round the till, and you could tell merely from their faces and dirty army boots that they'd just come down from the mountains. 'They can't be bothered to change their shoes', she comments.

And when an elderly person asked when he was going to get his pension, she goes on, the manager of the Pale branch of PBS replied: 'As soon as we're set up as a real bank.'

'And when will that be?' asked the old man

'In a few days, when we've finished Sarajevo off ', the manager replied, with a triumphant smile on his face.

The helicopter traffic over our house is growing denser and denser. What does this mean? They fly so low I feel I could almost touch them. There's more than one place in Pale where they can land: the football field, which is handy for the radio station and SRNA, and also for the Panorama and Turist hotels where officials of the new authorities are lodged; in front of Hotel Koran, which has now been turned into a hospital; and also the military base in Koran, which the JNA built right after 1945.

Naively and stupidly I wonder where they get the money for all these flights. My neighbour tells me that a blue B-H MUP helicopter landed on the football field yesterday, stolen of course, and the Serbs nearly shot it down themselves.

I watch the opening of the Seville world exhibition on TV, and remember promising my family last year that we'd certainly go and visit it. The exhibition lasts for a year. I wonder if there's any hope of our still being able to see it?

In the evening a mega-concert on TV in honour of the dead rock star Freddy Mercury and against AIDS. At least for a couple of hours forgot the darkness that surrounds me.

Pale, Tuesday 21 April 1992

'Wherever we're in control there's peace, and wherever the Muslims are there's war', the leader of the Bosnian Serbs announces today.

In Pale even the children play with submachine-guns stolen in Faletići, property of the Sarajevo Territorial Defence. It won't be long before they start being born with submachine-guns, all ready to shoot.

In Sarajevo they're distributing arms to defend the city.

In Pale Serb reservists are getting drunk on stolen whisky. By night they shoot at Muslim houses. A mad dance of our local barbarians. 'The Devil Unleashed' to a T.

22.00

Exactly. Tangible horror. The thunder of cannon is audible. I hear on Radio Sarajevo that they're shelling Old Town, where my son lives (he's not answering the phone, he must be in the cellar).

'There's no statute of limitation for war crimes', I say out loud in the empty house. When the day comes for trials, I'll be a witness.

If I come out alive I'll definitely leave Pale, and I'll never come back to the birthplace I've loved so dearly. Not for fear of being killed, but out of profound shame at living surrounded by murderers and thieves. The name Pale freezes the blood in the veins of people from Sarajevo, but it makes me want to vomit.

Pale, 22 April 1992

The day began at 1.30 when the shelling of Sarajevo stopped. It started up again at 5.30.

My son calls me at 13.30 to tell me I won't recognize Baščaršija when I see it. He spent the night in the cellar, counting the shells. By 22.00 eighty had fallen round their shelter.

A bird is singing in my garden, the street is empty, just stray dogs running around.

Every exploding shell that falls on the city and destroys it hurts me as if it were damaging my mind.

14.00

You can no longer hear the din from the hills separating Sarajevo from Pale. Are the killers resting, having lunch or getting drunk for another night's orgy?

19.30

The monster from Lapišnica (a large-calibre gun) comes to life again. I try to picture the faces of the people who feed it with deadly food and fire it at Sarajevo, where they went to school or first kissed a girl. Or are they perhaps like some sludge or mud oozing over this land, covering it and burying everything of value, all that has been created over hundreds of years? Is this the final victory of barbarism, that monstrous side of human nature that brings only death, over humanism?

Until a few days ago a car with powerful loud-speakers drove round the streets of Pale playing Serb national songs, especially ones accompanied on the *gusle*. That same car is now roaming the streets of Pale calling on people to give blood for the wounded 'heroes of Trebević'. Does blood too have nationality?

Today the helicopters are landing only on the pad in front of the hospital, which I can see from the terrace of my house. At night, when the rest of Pale is without electricity, only the hotel-hospital is lit up.

At every news report that many Serb fighters have been wounded or killed, the Muslims are 'scared to death' that tonight they may be massacred in revenge. I hear that the badly wounded are being taken by helicopter to Belgrade .

The garden – we plant garlic, onions and carrots.

Our friend M. brings us milk and cheese, asking discreetly if we have any food. Her son, who's a doctor, was forcibly conscripted on the first day and is taken to work at the hospital every day in a military jeep. A brilliant young man who specializes in internal medicine, he is now in despair. He is thinking of escaping. We find out that a regular bus route has been established to Belgrade. Two buses every morning, crammed with people running away via Pale to Serbia, Montenegro or beyond. The Army checks the passengers to make sure no one subject to the draft 'legs it'.

Our friend J.V. calls from Sarajevo and says: 'Come on, Daddy, tell them to start shooting!'

That's good. It's quiet. We laugh.

Pale, Thursday 23 April 1992

This morning at 5.30 I lie awake in bed and listen attentively to hear whether dawn will bring back the thunder of guns, the demolition of the city and the killing of its civilians.

Today Lord Carrington arrives in Sarajevo. What's he doing in our Balkan mountains, for God's sake, where a prescribed number of people *has* to die, to be killed, before passions can be stilled? How from his own world does he picture this world? Does he really think he can help it, that he will be understood at all here? A person drowning will clutch at a straw floating on the water, so I shall at this lord.

24.00

At noon today they 'signed a cease-fire', while this evening like a wild horde they're shelling and destroying Sarajevo. Dozens killed. Only one thing is certain – for a long, long time there'll be no end to this crime. A voice inside me keeps saying:' Go, go any way you can, what are you waiting for?', but another repeats Selimović's advice: 'So long as there's at least one reason not to go, don't go!'

3.00

Tomorrow, no today already, it is six years since Chernobyl, eight thousand dead and who knows how many permanently sick. Chernobyl or Bosnia, what's the difference?

A friend from Pale, who used to visit my house frequently, today hurries down the street dressed in army uniform. I realize that he has found himself, but lost me forever.

A friend from Sarajevo TV ('the eminent N.P.') rings me and says that they want to kill him. He asks me what he should do. Someone is offering him a flat and a job abroad.

> ... It is midnight. The rain is beating on the windows.
> It was not midnight. It was not raining...
>   Samuel Beckett, *Molloy*

Pale, Friday 24 April 1992

Orthodox Good Friday, a holiday on earth, two days before the resurrection of Christ. Normal, ordinary, working people know that perfectly well, but the Serb Radio in Pale explains to the Great Serbs what it means. Once the Great Communists used to explain in the same way to their people that there was no God. In Pale they're the very same individuals. They have rejected the old authorities and embraced the new, in order to extract some advantage from them.

A really rusty car with Dubrovnik plates goes by, packed with bearded, dirty figures.. I look too at how the famous sportsman K. drives around in his stolen BMW, now even more famous as the Holiday Inn sniper. For these people he's a hero, for those in the city he's a murderer. This war is a paradise for thieves and pathological killers.

The Muslims wander desolately around their 'bazaar', or stand in their courtyards with heads bowed, looking at the ground. They're still hoping that this will all stop, that it cannot get worse.

A morbid, painful evening.

Dr F. suddenly turns up at my house (like most other Ph.Ds he got his doctorate on an incredibly stupid topic, and it shouldn't have passed muster even as a matriculation essay). All he wrote in the past was the purest apologia for communism – and from the communists he got everything in return. Now he writes in defence of Islam. The other end of the stick that's now beating people on the head. He wipes his nose with his hand, then rubs it on his sleeve.

He wants me to 'declare myself'. What's worse, he smoked all our cigarettes, drank the last drop of spirits that we'd been eking out for days. His ideological mentor and personal friend, a great Marxist, well known intellectual and darling of communist politicians while they were in power, had changed his shirt even earlier and gone over to the party of the extreme right, then died despised by his old employers, celebrated by the new.

Why wonder that communism collapsed?

Already tipsy, Dr F. starts making play with our son's given name and my wife's background. She loses her temper and bluntly tells him what she thinks. F. is embarrassed and falls silent, since he didn't expect that. He leaves, and we're left feeling queasy at the thought that such people should even exist. If that fellow ever came to power, he'd be a tireless executioner in the name of 'his people'.

Pale, Saturday 25 April 1992

What will this day be like? It started off sunny.

Finally some limit is set. The 'renowned professor' Dr. Koljević appealed for the Serb cadres of Sarajevo TV to report and start working for 'the good of their nation'. Poor Doctor, he'd surely never heard there was any such thing as professional journalism. Via the screen he begged his legionaries to be calm tomorrow because of the holiday, and not to shoot or kill. He says how: 'the world must be shown our respect for the traditions of our forefathers'.

There's another reason for it though. The day after tomorrow, on Monday, the Third Yugoslavia is being announced in Belgrade. Serbia and Montenegro – like two eyes in a head. Is there any brain behind those 'eyes'?

Pale, Sunday 26 April 1992

Orthodox Easter. Once a normal, quiet, intimate family holiday for Orthodox believers in Christ. Today it's being celebrated by people who have as much in common with Jesus as did the Pharisees (for those who don't know: people who interpreted the Biblical message about loving thy neighbour as hatred for all who are foreign or different).

As I stand beside my father's grave and light a candle, a childhood friend (now in uniform) comes up to me and attacks me because of my film about the destruction of Dubrovnik. 'You fell for the ustasha lies', he says.[7]

His wife says: 'The only thing I hold against them (the people from Pale) is that they started bombarding Sarajevo before getting all the Serbs out!'

7.　The Ustasha (rebel) Croatian Revolutionary Organization, founded in fascist Italy in 1929 by Ante Pavelić, was installed in power in the so-called 'Independent State of Croatia' (NDH) – which covered most of Croatia and B-H – by the Axis occupiers in 1941. After the former Partisan Franjo Tuđman came to power in Croatia in 1990, he proclaimed his wish to reconcile the Partisan and Ustasha traditions; the latter enjoyed little public sympathy within Croatia, but was influential among returning emigrés and also had a base of support in Herzegovina. The term 'ustasha' (plural 'ustashe') came into general use by Serb nationalists to refer to all Croats, and by loyal Bosnians especially from 1993 on to refer to those Croats who supported Zagreb's aggressive policies towards B-H.

All morning volleys and sporadic rifle-shots in celebration of Easter echo round Pale. Still, not nearly as bad as it was last winter, for Christmas. Perhaps they're saving ammunition.

My wife uses our daughter's room upstairs as a lookout point. Perhaps she's scared of uninvited guests at night.

A car with powerful loudspeakers drives round Pale calling on people to stop shooting. I soon realize why: a long column of vehicles with foreign TV company markings is passing by the graveyard, from the direction of Jahorina. At the front and rear of the column, military and police cars for security.

Foreign journalists are supposed to find a real idyll of peace and happiness in Pale. It has to be shown how immaculately the new Serb authorities are functioning.

Journalists are really the biggest fools. They'll be sure to present them with some Muslim who'll say that no one is maltreating or oppressing him. While Stalin was killing thousands of people in Moscow, closed trucks circled the city with pictures of bread and the word for it in various foreign languages. Journalists reported on the excellent food supplies in Moscow. Those trucks contained prisoners on their way to the Ljubjanka. The pictures of old masters never fade. Disguised communists are now dancing to national music.

In the afternoon an army helicopter landed right in the centre of the football field in Pale, with a famous general and an even more famous Montenegrin politician, to start negotiations over the status of the JNA in B-H. Not far from the stadium, on an ordinary stretch of grass, children are playing football.

In front of the Orthodox church Serbs are gathering in their Sunday best, people who were once loyal servants of communism shunning church like the plague.

Who said: 'Everything flows, everything changes'?

I speak on the phone to my friend from RTVS and offer him five days in Pale in exchange for five minutes in Cafe Sarajevo with the crowd. He laughs and says: 'Thanks, but no thanks!'

I learn that a friend from Pale Z.B. (a Croat) was badly beaten up when he tried to get through by some side road from Sarajevo to Pale, where his family is.

Nobody asks *why*. Nobody answers *because*. Simply, a man has just been beaten almost to death and no questions are asked.

Pale, Monday 27 April 1992

Day of the ceremonial proclamation of the new Federal Republic of Yugoslavia.

I hear from an acquaintance at the council offices that there are 'lists of dishonourable Serbs to be liquidated'. My God, how arrogant and Stalinistic that sounds. Who compiles those lists, what kind of criteria are applied in selecting the people to be shot? Where is the court that pronounces the verdict, where are the lawyers and where the jury? Unbelievable. I realize that all totalitarian parties and governments have the word *democratic* in their titles. All round me I see democracy walking about in army boots with a submachine-gun on its shoulder. I see it flying through the skies, scaring the poor, little moles on the ground with the deafening sound of its propellers. I hear it reaching me through the earth's crust as the reverberation of cannon. Will I manage to survive such a quantity of democracy around me?

I see Meho making wooden shutters for his windows. He naively believes these will protect him when THEY knock on his door.

I also found out something quite unbelievable: Serbs who have exchanged their houses with Muslims are giving the exact coordinates and locations of their former homes to the gunners on Trebević, so that they'll be destroyed first.

We suspect they're listening in to our calls. We can't understand the 'music' on the telephone.

My wife ceremonially proclaims our garden the Independent Istrian Republic. She sits in the garden and studies prospectuses from San Marino.

Pale, Tuesday 28 April 1992

Difficult decision that our son MUST leave Sarajevo as soon as possible and head for the West, far away from this bestiality, and stay there perhaps for ever. I don't know if he'll succeed in passing through the gates of hell. He is classified purely as follows: given name Hrvoje, place of birth Rijeka, place of residence Pale, surname Vuksanović, tall and strong, hence a desirable warrior for any army, 'an unknown hero who gave his life for the freedom of his people'.

I rely on the friends from Sarajevo who are looking after him, and on God, to protect him from the checks and guards of assorted military formations. For any one of these, certain of his 'personal details' will be suitable, others will lead him to death. I'm worried and can think of nothing else.

Pictures of Istria constantly run through my thoughts, as a possible fragment of the earth's crust where, if we survive, we might all meet up and start something from scratch. I dream of it as a place where there are no 'nights of the long knives', where people bending over the red soil plant and harvest its fruits, where the very word 'politics' doesn't exist, or if it does exist is confined to the furthermost corner of the mind.

Here in my home town there is nothing more for me to seek. It will be hard to leave behind only the graves of my parents, the forested slopes of Jahorina and Romanija where I have walked and skied. Now those forests are full of killers who shoot at anything that moves and isn't 'a leaf from their mountain'. I know, I feel it, that one day – when all their leaves have fallen – they'll remain alone and naked to present their bloody accounts before God and man..

Not just national ghettoes are being created here, but something much worse: ghettoes for crooks, war criminals and profiteers.

I'm a bit shocked by the news – a rumour from Sarajevo – that 'if I'm still in Pale, then I'm certainly working for *them*'.

Is it still possible to explain to either side that I'm not working for anybody? That all I'm trying to do is save myself from the clutches of their madness? Still, I understand. To live in the suburbs of Auschwitz surrounded by executioners and not be with them is virtually impossible. Yet it is possible, the only question is for how long.

Pale, Wednesday 29 April 1992

Early this morning my wife managed to get a ride from Pale to Sarajevo in a military truck, in order to take our son his papers and see our daughter. Only women are able in this way to ride as far as Vraca, then walk down to the city – and this only when there's a let-up in the fighting. We found out about this way of getting into the city from S.R., who went like that to her mother's funeral in Vojkovići.

The Serb army has cut a forest track across the slopes of Jahorina, behind Trebević, so that 'travellers' won't see the positions from which Sarajevo is being shelled. By the main road via Lapišnica you used to get to Sarajevo in a quarter of an hour, whereas this roundabout route takes four or five hours. I fear for her life. My surname will 'save her', but her place of birth will 'sink her'.

When I started building this house in Pale ten years ago, I wanted it to be as big as possible, to have as many rooms as possible, so that friends from all over the country and from Sarajevo could come and visit us, for a rest or for the company. Now, for the first time, I feel a mysterious chill run through me as I move about the deserted house. It has so many big windows that I feel totally exposed to the gaze of the strangers around me.

My neighbours Meho and Đulzida ask me where my wife is, and when I tell them they ask me fearfully whether I shan't perhaps be leaving too. They feel somehow safer when I'm here. I wonder what sort of security I can give them, when I'm entirely powerless. Our close friend M. brings me some cheese pie and asks if I need anything else. She tells me fearfully that their attic is full of electronic equipment, rugs and other valuable things that their Muslim neighbours have brought over so that the Serb soldiers don't loot them. She tells me she's ashamed to be Serb. A wonderful human being, who sees everything and understands everything. She tells me that if I'm scared on my own I can move into their house, but at once corrects herself and says that if I leave the house empty they'll break in. I feel sorry for her. One of her sons managed to get away to America at the last moment, the other plans to do the same – but he has a two-year-old son and a one-month-old daughter. And as for herself, for whom should she work and for what should she hope, she asks me.

Pale, Thursday 30 April 1992

A shock that shakes me to the very core. This morning, when my son was supposed to get on a bus for the West, both bridges in Brčko were blown up. The road to the West no longer exists. I could go mad, howl like a dog, for not packing him off earlier. Didn't everything 'tell me' that at any moment the last umbilical cord offering salvation might snap? I blame myself for being stupid and blind, but it's too late now. All he can do now is hide out day and night in the cellar of the building in Old Town, hoping a shell does not get him. My wife tells me over the phone that last night he asked her: 'can your spine chatter from fear?' – something that he'd felt a few days earlier, when a shell exploded in their courtyard as they were running down to the cellar and all the glass from the windows showered down on them.

Tears come to my eyes, but I can't do anything now. Once again I ask myself whether I made a mistake in not bringing him to Pale, as my brother-in-law suggested. But no, a hundred times not to Pale! If he'd come here, they'd have taken him immediately, dressed him up in a uniform and sent him to Trebević to shoot at his friends. That would have been the end for both him and me. This way, at least there's hope.

I yell down the phone to my brother-in-law in Titograd, explaining to him that it's better for my son to be killed in Sarajevo by a shell fired by war criminals than to become a killer from Trebević. My brother-in-law can't understand this and hangs up on on me. My sister just cries.

What a nightmare. Separation of people into US and THEM , close friends and relatives turned into enemies.

At night I walk through the empty house questioning myself over and over again, but always repeating out loud: 'No, never, no'.

I have smoked my last cigarette and feel the panic of a nicotine addict seize me.

A dark, rainy night in Pale, thick as dough, with just one little, faraway window still lit. It reminds me of a still flickering hope. Like a dog I've shrunk into a corner beside the grate and am listening to Bach fugues.

' "Like a dog", said K. It was as if the shame would outlive him.' Franz Kafka, *The Trial.*

Pale, Friday 1 May 1992

May Day morning. From the day when, after 1945, this day became an institution that by order of the communists had to be celebrated, it became the saddest day of the year. Former communists in the new Federal Republic of Yugoslavia, who have now become socialists, ordain by decree that it once again must be celebrated. Along the main roads in Pale, on the SRNA building, the municipal offices, the police station, the hospital, Serb flags with their four S's flutter.[8]

The Muslims, who no longer leave their ghettoes, look at these flags and still hope it all is just ephemeral folklore. Why and by what right should I destroy the illusions of my neighbour Miralem and intensify his fear? Perhaps he is right, and not I.

This sad day in Pale is even sadder because nothing is working, apart from the black marketeers and the military machine. Only the twitter of birds in the garden brings solace.

---

8. The four seeming Cyrillic S's figuring on Serb national emblems are commonly interpreted as standing for *Samo Sloga Srbe Spašava* = Only Unity Saves the Serbs, but in fact derive from Byzantine motifs.

Pale, Saturday 2 May 1992

This morning I ask my neighbour what day it is. In the isolation of a ghetto a person loses any feeling for time, for days or hours. As if the future no longer exists, all is mere subsistence between morning and evening. A dark night serves only to train your senses, which are now as sharp as a dog's and register every little sound in and around the house.

Government and party leaders smuggle tankerfuls of petrol and tons of weapons, earning millions of DM in the process. Local bosses do it on the local level and earn hundreds of thousands of DM, and small-time black marketeers do it in their backyards, selling food and cigarettes, earning hundreds of DM. I hear that a pistol fight broke out between small-scale smugglers on the marketplace in Pale this morning, over some trucks full of cigarettes 'for the soldiers at the front'. Small and big black marketeers alike are protected by the police in Pale, because this makes for 'better market supplies in the free Serb territory'. Black marketeers drive proudly round Pale in expensive cars with no number plates. They are the true offspring of the new class of people that the 'new democratic government' is spawning.

'The dust shall return to the earth and the spirit unto God', says Jesus to his disciples.[9]

15.00

Terrible shelling of Sarajevo, all parts of it, especially the Centre neighbourhood. An hour ago the radio broadcast the news from Lisbon that: 'talks between the warring parties have been

---

9. The remembered quotation is in fact from the Old Testament book of Ecclesiastes.

suspended until hostilities cease'. The iron logic of war is relentlessly pulling the strings of a further and yet more bestial annihilation of all that men have created over hundreds of years. In panic I wonder what is happening to my family and friends in the city.

I always used to wonder about the kind of people who bombarded Dubrovnik. Is Sarajevo destined for a still worse fate? The fate of Beirut or Vukovar?

Who are these people who kill civilians in the city? Are they human at all, or just monsters who enjoy firing shells at woman, children, old people? My God, is this possible at all? Everything is possible here, a tiny, desperate voice within me whispers.

I try in vain to get through to my family in Sarajevo. The unbearable music on the telephone lines is driving me crazy. Two worlds (once one) only fifteen km. apart: one dies, suffers, weeps, the other shoots, plays music and sings.

The Serb radio has just reported that: 'not a single shell has been fired at Sarajevo from Lapišnica (Pale)'. As I listen to this, I hear the muffled thunder of guns from the direction of Lapišnica. These people are the quintessence of falsehood, their very being is falsehood.

The most terrible day, evening and night in Sarajevo. My God, is this the peak of Golgotha, can this horror still grow, go further? What is further, what does it look like?

22.00

I walk through the dark house like an animal in a cage, while the windows rattle slightly from the gunfire on Trebević and

Lapišnica. If they're rattling here, what kind of hell must it be in Sarajevo?

Pale, Sunday 3 May 1992

All telephone communications with Sarajevo and 'the world' severed. Is my family alive, my friends, all the decent people?

Jesus says: 'Forgive them, Father, for they know not what they do.' My God, how can I forgive them or convince myself that they don't know what they're doing. I doubt I'll ever again set foot in their New Land, though I have lots of friends and relations there.

You don't feel your hand or leg until it starts hurting, it's the same with the telephone. Now that it doesn't work it's as though I'm totally cut off from 'the outside world'.

All that exists is this ghetto I live in, and the despair I feel because of it. Before I could at least hear familiar voices, listen to their fears and hopes, absorb them into myself and carry them with me as my most precious possession. I was part of them. Now I'm completely alone.

I learn that the new authorities have decided to dismiss the brilliant manager of a hotel on Jahorina because he's 'partly ustasha'. In other words, his wife's mother is from somewhere in Croatia.

My weekly visit to my mother's grave suddenly becomes something odd, abnormal. They watch me with suspicion and mistrust. The stonemason who did the final work on her gravestone last year asks me why *obitelj* is written on the gravestone rather than *porodica*,[10] why my mother is buried here and not next to my father in the Orthodox graveyard, and why I visit the graveyard every week, when nobody else does so. He questions me as though he has the right, as a 'pure-blooded Serb', to ask anything he wants. He now has an 'attitude towards me', whereas a couple of years ago he just kept quiet, worked and took his fee.

I learn from a childhood friend, who has remained the same in spite of the new regime, that the old cinema has been turned into a prison.

He tells me: 'Stubborn Serbs who don't want to go to Trebević are tied to radiators and beaten until they themselves start begging to go to Trebević.

I learn that another friend of mine, a skiing enthusiast, wants to disown his son, who keeps repeating: 'Sarajevo must be turned into a potato patch!'

In Pale, joints of veal are brought on the hoof to 'distinguished Serbs in authority', with the recipient's name written on the meat. I remember my parents saying how after Liberation the same kind of joints were brought for 'distinguished communists', but packed in cardboard boxes. The Pale lot are poor pupils of the old bosses.

On TV a report about Alija Izetbegović being imprisoned in the military barracks near the Airport. I discover the shocking incapacity of him and his associates finally to grasp what is really going on.

---

10.   Although the distinction between *obitelj* and *porodica* is properly that between nuclear and extended family, the former is a typically Croatian usage, whereas the latter would be normal in a Serbian Orthodox context.

There are fewer and fewer lit windows in Pale, more and more darkness. Perhaps this darkness is our lasting destiny.

Pale, Monday 4 May 1992

I listen to the early morning news. Shells are falling on the southern part of Sarajevo. New fighting in Doboj, in Brčko It's now becoming quite clear that they're going for a military solution and the seizure of B-H territory by force of arms, regardless of the death toll. Talks with the UN will come later.

A fatal mistake that I didn't send my son out earlier. Now he's squatting with his sister and mother in a cellar near the Princip bridge, counting the shells. O God, are they alive and have they got anything to eat? How do I overcome this quiet despair, which is destroying me and growing ever louder?

In Pale a total mobilization is taking place of all Serbs between 16 and 60. I hide my diary in a cavity behind the fireplace. The mere act of written or verbal condemnation of their crime is enough for the executioners to come for me.

Scene from Pale: a 'proper Serb', a childhood comrade, popped into my garden to say: 'It's not good that Sarajevo's being shelled, but because of them (the Muslims) life had become impossible.'

Another 'proper Serb', a lawyer, says to me: 'When I was young, I asked my father why the Turks had oppressed us for five hundred years, and he answered: "because we didn't pay them back properly"; now they're going to be paid back in full', says the lawyer, and rides off on his bicycle.

The helicopter traffic has become so dense and regular that I can tell the time by it.

I can't watch Sarajevo TV programmes any longer. The relay station on Hum has been shelled.

This destructive, heavy, muffled firing from Lapišnica and Trebević, which doesn't stop for a moment, will wreck me for the rest of my life. I can understand that on both sides there are pure criminals, killers, pathological types thirsty for blood, but I absolutely cannot understand at all how people fire deadly shells from the surrounding hills at ordinary, wretched civilians.

My neighbour Meho tells me today: 'There's no life here any longer.'

I tell him that there is, but for killers and war criminals.

Pale, Tuesday 5 May 1992

My God, is it possible that the war has been going on for a month already? It's not possible. A morning without electricity or telephone. I haven't got the most important thing in these circumstances: an ordinary little transistor radio.

The electricity comes on and I find out that the Serbs have 'liberated part of Dobrinja', as SRNA reports. In order to understand this a person would really have to be completely mad.

There is now a telephone connection with Sarajevo only with numbers starting with 5 or 6. The splendid post office building on the Obala, in which I used to feel like a civilized being, proud that such a building should exist in Sarajevo, has now been destroyed by shells. It survived two World Wars, and now the barbarians have reduced it to ashes in a month. All connections with the Old Town and Centre neighbourhoods have been destroyed. The journalist M.J. from Sarajevo TV calls me to say that the death toll is in hundreds. One woman is lying dead under some fallen branches. For hours already no one has been able to move her because of snipers.

With relief I learn that my family is alive.

Another night falls over Pale. I can hear fierce shooting from the nearby woods. In this 'liberated territory' someone is nevertheless fighting for freedom.

In my thoughts I follow the path of a shell and see my friend, a painter, huddled into some corner waiting for it to fall on him.

Mina comes every day to ask after my wife (she says she feels better when she's here) and to phone her sister in Alipašino Polje. She has a fifteen-year-old daughter and two sons. Impossible to tell which of them she's more worried about. I see fear in her eyes.

Pale, Wednesday 6 May 1992

Another dawn breaks. I lie in bed and look through the big window at how the twilight fades and the first ray of sunlight illuminates Pale. How nothing has changed for thousands of years, and how nevertheless in this past month everything has changed.

One more truce signed, one more 'cease-fire', and one more despicable shelling of Sarajevo.

I'm starting to talk out loud to the dogs and to myself. Once I used to be irritated by the noise my wife and children made, now I long for it.

A 'renowned' doctor and politician from Sarajevo, who was among the first to transfer to Pale and take a ministerial seat in the new Serb regime, comes to my yard with his new partner, a journalist from Radio Sarajevo, and asks about my house. I look dreadful from hunger and lack of sleep. I tell them they can't 'move in with me'. Their uniformed bodyguard and driver watches me carefully. I cannot understand his partner at all, who left behind in the city her old mother and her friends, to be shelled by these people with whom she now associates. The human being is an impossible being.

This visit scares me. It's easy to be brave in the movies. A tide of nausea, sorrow and hopelessness rises within me.

The dog constantly fidgets round my legs, ingratiating itself, as though lacking company.

Pale, Thursday 7 May 1992

It can't be Thursday already. Is there any point in registering it or living through it at all.

Today a convoy of trucks goes round Sarajevo collecting the dead. Where will they put them, when the mortuaries are overflowing and you can't get to the cemetery. They bury them in the parks. Which day was it, when a doctor was giving out instructions on burial over the radio? 2m. long, 1m. wide, 2m. deep, 50 m. away from walls and water or sewage pipes. Together with the corpse, bury any known personal details. If there's no wooden box, at least use a plastic sheet.

A springlike, sunny, warm, hopeless day, like the death stalking Sarajevo. I'm unable to think, when I hear that a sniper has killed a three-year-old little girl.

In this darkness, a distant, familiar voice by some miracle finds its way through to me, bringing hope and happiness.

A whole arsenal of weapons has been found in TV producer M.T.'s Sarajevo flat, so he makes a statement from Pale for the Sarajevo TV news programme, saying that he's not a terrorist, but was just endangered.

What a lie. Nobody was endangering him while he was doing what he liked on television. With trepidation I await his next visit.

On the big wall clock, which no longer works, I've covered the hands to make me feel that someone's thinking about me all the time.

'This is a *šljivovica* war', says a European diplomat, sipping Martel brandy.

Pale, Friday 8 May 1992

All day I do nothing but think frenetically about how to get my son and daughter 'across the border'. I analyse thousands of combinations and each one collapses like a house of cards. Now it's too late for anything. Why was I so stupid and waited so long?

Pale, Saturday 9 May 1992

How absurd: with my neighbour Meho, who's a craftsman, I've been putting shutters over my windows. I haven't put them up for the past five years, and now I'm doing so as if this will save me from the 'outside world'. Meho is a happy man, because he has learnt always to be working at something. I see his fear growing day by day. He lives in Pale with his wife, while his daughter and her children live in Sarajevo. When there was no electricity for a week, he threw away a vast amount of food he'd been keeping in the freezer for his daughter. He doesn't get his pension. He says that at the bank they give money only to Serb refugees from the city, but tell him the money hasn't arrived yet. His son went to America a few years ago, but can't send him money at present. The whole of Meho's life, invested in his house and garden, is now collapsing.

Today is Victory over Fascism Day. In Europe and the rest of the world, but not here. Here fascism is being reborn and taking its toll of blood. The Balkans seem to me like an accursed fragment of the earth's crust where day occasionally dawns only for night to fall again.

My friend N.P., a producer at Sarajevo TV, escaped this morning on a military plane for Belgrade, and then on to England. In Sarajevo they're calling him a traitor. I don't know, I can't judge because I don't have proper information about what was really happening to him.

It's night. I sit outside my house and look at the unlit buildings in which people are living or dying. They look like the graveyard memorials of a certain time, a horrible time. Night-time is the hardest here in Pale, it's as if all the horror of the day is condensed into it, to let a man know by its intensity that he is nothing, perhaps just some phantom in the darkness anxiously awaiting the dawn.

Pale, Sunday 10 May 1992

Another sunny day. Will it be dreadful?

10.00

I go to the graveyard. The road is empty and I see people watching me through half-open windows. Everything has stopped, petrified in expectation of something that is just about to arrive. In the graveyard the fresh mound of a man from Dubrovnik who came to visit his family in Pale 'before the war' and died here. Another fresh grave – this belongs to a young man, a local, who suddenly died of a heart attack. He used to cut the grass in the graveyard and keep it tidy.

I tell myself once again that God knew this was going to happen, so he took my mother three years ago.

Once I used to go for a walk in the woods after the graveyard. Now I don't dare.

12.00

Like a hungry dog waiting for someone to throw it a gnawed bone, I wait for news on the radio, to learn whether those who cannot agree at all have come to any agreement.

The news begins: 'The criminal destruction of B-H and Sarajevo is continuing. What is happening all round us is worse than the blackest Fascism!'

A good childhood friend comes into my garden, Dado, a maths teacher at the primary school. A decent man, who wouldn't hurt a fly. He drains the offered cognac at a gulp. I know it must be hard for him, far harder than for me. He tells me how, instead of the answers to his homework, a pupil just writes SDS in block capitals in his notebook. He gives him a pass mark, since anything else is tantamount to suicide. He's still hoping that all this will end, that he won't lose his job and have to leave Pale. He has two small sons, who play in the garden without a care. I think of my childhood, when I too played without a care though in 1944 war was raging all round me.

Helicopters fly low above our heads with a deafening clatter and land on the football field. Dado leaves and I remain alone. I think about my son, my daughter and my wife in Sarajevo. They can be killed by a shell and I won't know, I can be killed here and they won't know. How is this to be borne?

If that black prediction comes true about the Serbs' crazy idea of cutting Sarajevo into two parts near the Marshal Tito barracks, then there will be thousands of deaths. There are soldiers with their families in the barracks, waiting for the outcome of the talks. They have become hostages of a monstrous idea about ethnically pure regions. From the barracks to Baščaršija should be the 'Turkish' (Muslim) part of the city, according to the SDS notion,, whilst the south as far as Ilidža should be Serb. In comparison to this, Beirut is child's play.

A childhood friend passes along the road, D., a lawyer, in uniform. He stops, comes up to me and complains that they haven't given him a 'proper' uniform, but an ordinary one of the kind night watchmen wear. He was given a submachine-gun, which he carries proudly over his shoulder, but no belt to stick his pistol in. He was a child of communism, now he's a child of the blackest nationalism.

This is a time that exposes people totally, their make-up is off and their lies show their true face. It's a face that frightens me.

My God, how unbelievably quickly the days pass! They're all the same, only the despair is different.

Pale, Monday 11 May 1992

A night of terror. With my head on the pillow, I can hear from the direction of Trebević and Lapišnica the dull roar of the howitzers 'razing Sarajevo to the ground'.

During the night my friends P.K. and M.J., Sarajevo journalists, telephone me to say that only over their dead bodies can the criminals from the forests conquer the city. Some of our Sarajevo TV or café friends are among those criminals. Once we all hung out together, now they're killing their friends. How is that possible? What has happened within us and around us? If it's true, and every shell fired carries the message that this is the terrible, inexorable truth, then the whole of our life spent with them was an illusion. The coming week will be the worst for people in the city. How can I help my family and friends?

A day like the most horrible dream, a nightmare of unanswered questions. Analysing a thousand possibilities of salvation means that the thousand and first will happen, the one leading to disaster.

Hunger and disease are beginning to haunt Sarajevo.

Meho and Miralem are digging the garden and planting vegetables, in the hope that they'll be picking them in the autumn. Mina keeps asking when my wife will be back from Sarajevo, so that she'll have someone to talk to. They know far more than me about what's happening in Pale and the surrounding villages. But they think that I know far more about events in the city and the world.

Pale, Tuesday 12 May 2001

Almost the entire night shifting places beside my bed. I can't put my head on the pillow, since the earth's crust is an exceptional conductor of sound – of the roar of cannon. How can a man sleep at all if he hears the firing of shells, if he imagines their flight to some house in Sarajevo, and sees it collapse, and bodies are left beneath the ruins? O God, can a human being understand at all another person's pain and death?

Today is the Orthodox Saint Basil Ostroški's Day, the day when my mother, though a Catholic, always sent money to Ostrog monastery (Montenegro), for our salvation and that of all righteous people. Now I truly realize how my parents, with their different faiths, were just a spark of light in this Balkan darkness.

My friends telephone me to say that my daughter and my wife left Old Town yesterday on their way to Ilidža, with the aim of reaching Pale by way of side roads. My son must on no account come to Pale, since they would immediately conscript him and send him to Trebević. Now I'm literally dying of fear, thinking of their journey. Will I see my son before he 'goes out into the world'? If he ever does go.

No wife or daughter in the afternoon, nor in the evening. What has happened to them? In the city there's a bit of a lull. I hope they're alive.

Pale, Wednesday 13 May 1992

Slight respite when I learn that the Serbs have decided on a 'five-day cease-fire'.

A happy moment has finally knocked on my door. T.S., a young woman who used once to work for SA-3 where I was the editor for a while, came to see me with her sister D.[11] They arrived from Sarajevo a little while ago to see their parents who live in Vučja Luka.

S. looks me straight in the eye and asks: 'I know you refused to work for SRNA. They met me on the street today and asked when I was going to start working for them. What do you advise?'

---

11.   SA-3 was the third channel of TV Sarajevo.

An incredible energy radiates from her tiny body. She was as if made for the camera, and used to dominate the studio simply by her appearance and eloquence. I thought very highly of her. I remained silent.

'I know what you think. Sorry for asking; I've already refused', she replies quickly.

But that wasn't the only reason for their visit, the other was the telephone in my house, that instrument of salvation which perhaps only in wartime gains its full value. Admittedly there's a public telephone booth in Pale, but it's always taken and in addition 'everyone can hear what you say' – and their boyfriends are Muslim.

Up until a few months ago, that was a normal thing. Now it's a mortal sin. National identity is becoming fateful for many loves, marriages and friendships. Now everything has shattered. I see and feel how much these two girls are suffering.

They flitted to the telephone like butterflies. They weren't bothered even by the unbearably loud music from the receiver, broadcast by the Radio of the Serb Republic of B-H.

I go into the garden to be out of their way. When I get back they look like drowned birds. They have suddenly realized that those fifteen kilometres separating them from their boyfriends seem like fifteen light years. They have categorically rejected all the rational reasons for staying safely with their parents in Vučja Luka, and are determined to go back to the city. They're now 'analysing the situation' with their boyfriends of how to get into Sarajevo. How dear these two young human beings are to me. They bring with them hope that not everything has sunk into hopeless darkness.

I give them Czesław Miłosz's book *The Captive Mind*, and also some 'light reading'.

'Read, just read', I tell them, 'that's the best way to defeat insanity.'

How happy I am! Spoke with my family over the phone. They're alive and looking for a way, any way, out of the Sarajevo hell.

The Serb authorities in Pale are compiling a census of all houses and flats. First Muslim and Croat ones. They're resettling the refugees who come to Pale in droves. I expect them to get round to me.

After a long time spoke on the telephone to V., a good friend and colleague from work, and told him to send his ill mother over to my place. A lovely, delicate, subtle woman – I can't imagine how she's enduring all this horror. I can't decide whom to feel most sorry for: newborn babies, mothers, children, young men and women, or the elderly. For every one of them, a powerful, merciless force has destroyed all their reality, all their dreams.

The girls have gone and I'm alone again in the house, which reminds me of a coffin.

Pale, Thursday 14 May 1992

Dreadful. The heaviest shelling so far of the city and the bloodiest battles on its surrounding slopes. With gun in hand or without, the young men rush off to Mojmilo, Vraca, the Jewish graveyard...The blood freezes in my veins at the scenes I see on the TV screen.

SRNA gives its version of the battle: 'It's a jihad!'. Everything that's not Serb is a jihad for them.

I call TV Sarajevo and my colleague K.B. tells me that the people of Sarajevo have opted for all or nothing. They've already captured some enemy strongholds.

In the dark, frozen sky a full moon is shining. Is all of this not its curse? A night of vampires who suck the blood of babies? I walk round the house like a phantom and pray to God for my children and my wife. Fear has totally paralysed me.

An aerial bombardment of Sarajevo is announced for tomorrow. Is that possible? If this war, this attack on Sarajevo was possible, then that's possible too.

Lit up by the moonlight Pale looks ghostly. On the road, men armed to the teeth walk up and down, 'keeping the peace of the faithful'. I must be dreaming.

Pale, Friday 15 May 1992

Is it possible that Friday has dawned?

12.00 News. 'BH is repelling the bestial attacks of the aggressor. Sarajevo is a ruined city...'

Muslims are asked to hand in their weapons, 'in the interest of their own security'. Groups of two or three 'officials' accompanied by an armed soldier walk round Pale compiling lists of people, property, animals. My mother told me they did the same immediately after liberation in 1945.

Agitated call from my friend M.J. at the TV, begging me to find out somehow what has happened to our friend N.K., who has been 'taken prisoner by the Serbs'. He is worried about him, that they might kill him, because he's a decent man.

What a shock. I watch him on Serb television having a polite and friendly chat with the editor I.G., who was once a feather in the cap of the communists, and in their name used to pass sentence before trial from the TV screen on people of 'his nation'. Now he thunders away on SRNA. Our colleague N.K., about whom we were all so concerned, is perfectly fine. He says he came over to the Serb side voluntarily and now wants to work for them. He's going off to Serbia in a military helicopter to visit his family, after which he'll 'involve himself actively in their work'.

My God, how false human beings are. Any one of us would have thrust their hand into the fire for him, yet how cheaply he sold himself.

M.J., who was so worried about him, now yells down the phone that some day he'll kill him with his own hands. We feel terribly deceived, and ashamed.

Pale, Saturday 16 May 1992

A Saturday morning like any other. What day, date or hour it is no longer has any importance. Everything has turned into naked duration, without beginning or end.

An editorial colleague of mine from TV Sarajevo cries and screams down the telephone, because our distinguished colleague N.A, the winner of many awards for ecological programmes, is in an Ilidža prison. She tells me to call up SRNA, the TV and all the rest in Pale, to explain to them that 'the Serbs don't have the right to arrest our colleagues merely because they're Muslim and live in Ilidža'.

How deluded she is. What does she think, who am I and how much power do 1 have, that I could explain this to people to whom absolutely nothing can be explained.

My colleague M.J. continues to curse and weep, exhorting a people to be 'honourable', and she's not even aware that such words have been utterly erased from the place where I live. I try to calm her down by telling her I'll 'do all I can'. To be in Pale, even in the kind of isolation I'm in, means to some people in Sarajevo that 'you're after all one of them and work for them'. I understand and don't blame them. One day, if I survive, we'll look each other in the eye.

I learn that it's a little quieter in the city today, and my wife and daughter will come . I 'see' their journey through the ruined city, their crossing of the bridge near Hotel Bristol – the bridge where they're a moving target for some maniac killer – the request for their papers and the checking of them in Grbavica which is held by the Serbs, their entry into the truck, the macadam road via Kasindo and the northern slopes of Jahorina, their arrival in Pale. I 'see' that journey, and see the chetniks with their cockades as they allow them through or hold them. I whisper: 'Let them just get through, and after that get away from Pale as soon as possible.' Women can still leave.

12.00 The News.

Total war in Sarajevo. Firing at all buildings, at civilians, from all military barracks.

Every hope for peace is actually one big illusion. Every announcement of a cease-fire one big lie.

15.30

My wife and daughter finally arrive in Pale. What joy. Pale strikes them as incredibly strange, alien, peaceful.

My daughter has spent almost a month in Dobrinja and Old Town, my wife half that time. And she left for just two days. They're full of impressions, so I beg them to note them down for me.

Recollections of Jadranka Vuksanović

These are my wife's recollections:

Wednesday 29 April 1992

A number of men and women climbed aboard the truck along the way; from their conversation I find out that they often go to Sarajevo, or rather to Vraca, from where the Serb army evacuated them. Now they live in other people's weekend cottages in the forest, their houses in Vraca have been transformed into artillery nests. They go to Sarajevo to collect as many of their belongings as they can. On the way, a few army checkpoints: the Pale ID card and the surname get me through. The passengers have noticed that the journey is getting better and better: a month ago it used to take up to twelve hours, now we arrive in Vraca at eleven in the morning. I'm stunned by the quantity of arms and soldiers, and by the appearance of once tame Vraca. I burst into the house of my friend M.J. in Grbavica. Her windows are blacked out with blankets. She laughs when I jump at every shot near the house. She's already used to it, she says: 'It's just the stocking-heads training, they all jump into a troop-carrier and go on a wild ride round Grbavica, shooting at all the surrounding windows.'

Accompanied by shooting we run across the bridge near the Natural Sciences and Mathematics Faculty, then take the tram to the centre of town. I look at the burnt out Unioninvest building. She goes to work, I continue to the Princip bridge.

I hug the children. They look fine. In the afternoon I go and pick up some money from Š.D., and arrange with her for her mother-in-law with the granddaughter and my son to travel together to Brčko. I'm near the Cathedral when there's a sudden burst of gunfire, all the customers sitting in the nearby cafés rush frantically for shelter. Most of them take out pistols, women shout: 'Kill him, kill!' They lead a young man in a track-suit from a front entrance, passers-by hit him, everyone says he's the sniper who was shooting. I'm left with the painful impression that it was actually some local settling of accounts – as I gathered from the comments of the people present. Telephone arrangements about our son's departure tomorrow; we're all packed and waiting for the dawn. A night punctuated by bursts of machine-gun fire and distant shelling.

Thursday 30 April 1992

The first morning news, and paralysis: the bridge in Brčko has been blown up. What now? Until we come up with something, we go shopping and to the High Commission for Refugees, for a paper that should enable my husband to get to Sarajevo.

We buy coffee and food. The market is wretchedly empty. People walk around, full of a certain pride. I meet acquaintances, we all hug each other, there's a kind of new comradeship. I go off to Šipad, I'm shocked by the appearance of my ruined office. A hole as big as a watermelon in the wall and the radiator. In the afternoon, around 16 h., I return from a café where I met many common friends, it's going to rain, there's no longer a living soul on the streets. 'Pale Alone in the World.'[12] People are already safe in their shelters.

---

12.   Pun on the title of a 1942 children's book, *Palle Alone in the World* by Jens Sigsgaard: Palle becomes Pale in Bosnian.

Entry gates are being locked, constant check on comings and goings. S. and J.M. live right across the street from the military HQ, a very awkward location, open space – the Miljacka, the Tsar Dušan park. I sleep fitfully.

Friday 1 May 1992

I go with J.V. to the market near Zetra – there's nothing there but pasta, seed onions, cigarettes, detergent. We laugh at how yesterday J.M. thought ordinary thunderclaps were shells, though there wasn't any shelling at all yesterday. Not in our part of town at least. I suggest she plants some onions, she's surprised you can do that in a pot. I'm in a constant panic about food. Outside her house I see a flowering dandelion, and explain to her how this is actually the 'rocket' being sold for so much money in the market. I show her what nettles are, all of which you can eat. Now she's upset, because they were dreaming about fresh greens and she had some there outside her window.

In the evening they suddenly start 'raining some down' nearby. Now I'm not comfortable staying in the flat either. For the first time, I go down to the cellar. A large one, from Austro-Hungarian times. Just one improvised bench near the coal. Not many of the residents, two quiet little children, their mother and their father who guards the front entrance with his rifle, three elderly ladies, one of their husbands, S., myself, my children. It's cold, everyone's wearing winter clothes. The shells fall so close that the thick, stone walls shake. Late at night Vijeko bursts in, the son of a pensioner who lives in the attic. He has skipped through the familiar courtyards to report that Baščaršija is on fire, and there's hand-to-hand fighting in Skenderija. H. is shaking with fear. B. is weeping, later she says she was weeping for Baščaršija. When the shelling stops, we gather our courage, return to the flat and try to get to sleep in our clothes.

Saturday 2 May 1992

A shock when I've got up enough courage to go outside. Baščaršija demolished, burnt out shops, glass, glass, glass, holes in the houses, mortar dust floats in the air, display windows shattered or with shrapnel holes, supermarkets already 'swept clean'. We buy sugar, I keep bumping into acquaintances, who ask after Mladen. Because of some sudden shelling we run home.

In the afternoon, at 16 h., I stealthily watch the announced pull-out of the army from the military HQ. The foliage in the park is green already, so you can't see very well, and they also warn me to get away from the window, because snipers 'see' infra-red rays. I suddenly notice in the channel of the Miljacka, under a bridge, a group of around twenty young men, dressed in assorted colours and armed. Every moment, when I come to the window and cautiously peep through, they're getting closer and closer to the HQ. I sense some dreadful evil, since it has been requested that the pull-out be completely secure. The young men hide behind trees, just like in films about the Partisans, but they're closer and closer to the HQ. A column of olive-green trucks starts moving off slowly, and you can see UN vehicles as well. Soon you can hear firing. What's happening? Later, on TV, we listen to Kukanjac and Kljujić arguing about whether there was shooting or not. It's true that there weren't any uniformed local forces, but it's also true that there was some shooting.

In the evening the vampire ball begins, just as we thought it was going to be peaceful. M.J hasn't come back home, so S. is terribly worried. It's a madhouse outside, I think there's street-fighting and they're actually firing in the entrance to our building. I smoke my first cigarettes since February. In a corner of the cellar, beer bottles with Molotov cocktails are ready. Vijeko and his father burst into the cellar to tell us that the Statistics building is on fire, on the other side of a shared courtyard. Panic grows, because where do we go if the fire spreads? We call the fire brigade, the cellar is getting warmer and warmer. With a short hose men water the roof of a small garage in the courtyard. From the stairway you can see that the flames are terrible. Luckily the wind isn't blowing in our direction. We can hear the fire brigade, but we also hear that the main Post Office building is on fire, and who knows what else.

Sunday 3 May 1992

We don't dare go out. M.J. arrives, he spent the whole night in the Paragraf Cafe, right by the Post Office.

There's no bread. We bake some from the last kilo of flour. We eat bread and lard.

Monday 4 May 1992

I borrow a little flour from my friend Š.D., she gives me some sugar and pasta too. M.V. offers to buy some food from the TV building. Some kind of desire to help radiates from people, so I just don't feel alone.

Wednesday 6 May 1992

The shelling is obviously devised by someone who wants to destroy people psychologically. Just when you're hoping that everything's peaceful at last, they 'rain down' a few shells right nearby; and just when you're preparing yourself for the vampire show, you hear nothing but silence for a few hours.

I think that was the day I ran across the Princip Bridge and finally bought some bread. I understand how fear of hunger is stronger than fear of bullets. What joy to have bread for tomorrow as well.

Thursday 7 May 1992

Meeting with a distant cousin, a lovely old gentleman, who advises me to try and secure my son's departure through the Jewish Community. He too is on their list, but because of his gravely ill wife he probably won't travel.

Friday 8 May 1992

We've put our son on the Jewish Community list. A new hope for his departure. He has to be permanently ready, since he'll be informed half an hour before departure. The flight will be free, which at least lessens my worries.

I plan my return to Pale, I call M.J. in Grbavica, on the other side of the city, I check on the situation, but everything changes from one moment to the next. When it's quiet here, all hell breaks loose in Grbavica. And vice versa. There's no bread again.

Sunday 10 May 1992

We sleep in our clothes, constantly ready for the cellar. I begin the day by listening to the radio, in order to find out whether I can leave the house in search of food. I'm overcoming my fear of open space. I know by now that the bullet I can hear definitely hasn't hit me. The one that does hit me, I shan't be able to hear. Today I get from M.V. some flour, beans and other food. My mood improves at once. I keep counting my children's mouthfuls, it seems to me they're hungry all the time. We have only one meal a day, but make do by drinking sugarless tea and eating bread and lard. Perhaps I'll manage tomorrow to get to Grbavica.

Monday 11 May 1992

No hope of leaving. Bought bread.

Wednesday 13 May 1992

I realize I can't visit even friends who live two (former) tram stops away. It's very dangerous to walk around, since you never know where or when things will start to 'grunt' – everyone uses this expression. Went to see B.R., ask her if my son can move over to their place, so that he'll be closer to the Jewish Community when the moment for evacuation comes. My son eats a fried egg after a long time. Wonderful people, they give me a slab of bacon, they're not as unprepared for hunger as S. and J.M.

Meeting with some of my husband's colleagues, a lovely day outside Café San [Dream], they're full of optimism and wit, I forget that hell is all around us. We phone home. Race for bread across the Princip bridge, between two attacks by those psychopaths from the hills.

We're packed, and waiting for a peaceful day to leave. I can't go on explaining to my daughter that we're using up our friend's precious food.

Friday 15 May 1992

Finally on our way. Around noon a TV van drives us at break-neck speed down the empty street; in front of the Marshal Tito barracks everyone gets down on the floor. Masses of people are killed here by snipers. We jump out of the van near the Hotel Bristol, pass through the checkpoints of the territorial defence units, then cross a small wooden bridge. A person grows so accustomed to rifle shots, machine-gun bursts, the thunder of artillery that he scarcely thinks about them.

I sense a terrible change in Grbavica, now with the emptiness of death, even though SRNA goes on about life being normal on the 'free' territory. Only the occasional face peering from an entrance.

We spend the night at M.J's, because we were late for the last bus to Pale, as they tell us at the Serb 'crisis centre'. I'm surprised, only ten days have gone by and instead of just military trucks, buses are already being used as well. Lj.J. turned quite green with fear because the Crisis HQ wanted to detain him for conscription. Only when they find out he's not a Serb do they let him go.

M.J. tells us about a nightmare she experienced a couple of days ago, when two drunken soldiers burst into their flat, threatening to slaughter her if they found an image of Our Lady. While she sat paralysed, they quickly turned the flat upside down, then still threatening went off to the neighbours' place on the same mission. All the residents are becoming more and more scared of the rampaging army that surrounds them, and that is already moving into abandoned flats. M. and Lj. think they must soon move from this part of town to that held by the B-H territorial defence forces. They'll exchange flats with our mutual friends, the O.s.

Saturday 16 May 1992

An old, sick couple, she in her night-gown, three young women being seen off by weeping mothers, we wait for the van to Tilava.

In Tilava we wait for three hours for a convoy of trucks heading for Sarajevo to go past. Some are jam-packed with bags of flour. Booming folk music blares from the trucks. There's also a kind of hospital there, helicopters land and take off — leaving behind empty, blood-stained stretchers.

Finally we get aboard a troop carrier full of very young Serbian soldiers. And this at a time when Karadžić has made statements claiming that not a single 'Serbian soldier has remained in Bosnia'. They're all the same age as my son. One of the soldiers, who is made sick by the jolting, they nickname 'the Bosnian'. At last we arrive in Pale.

Pale Diary

16 May to 15 July 1992

My diary continues:

Late in the afternoon, my daughter goes out to visit acquaintances and friends in Pale. She returns home and says she'd rather go back to Sarajevo straight away. She'll go crazy here. Now she realizes what it has been like for us.

I learn that two people I knew from Sarajevo TV have been killed.

Pale, Sunday 17 May 1992

An incredibly beautiful Sunday morning. I lie in my bed and think of all the possible and impossible ways to go to Sarajevo tomorrow, or the day after, and try to get my son out via Ilidža to Split.

A friend from the TV, M. (a lighting specialist), calls me up in tears. Some friends of his age have been killed right in front of their own house, near Hadžići. He asks me what to do, where to go and what side to join? He doesn't want to join anyone, he doesn't want to kill anyone. His village is Serb, but he never cared who was what, and now he's supposed to shoot at his Muslim friends. He doesn't want to shoot, he just wants to save himself from this madness. I understand him, but my reassurance that all this will pass is of no great help to him. Any more than it is to me.

A late night phone call from the producer M.T., who's now in Pale working heart and soul for SRNA. I'm gripped by anxiety that he may just say: 'I'll come right over to your place.'

He knows, and I know, that he can come whenever he wants to, that I'm powerless in front of him, just a word from him is enough to finish me off.

Luckily he doesn't announce a visit, instead merely says triumphantly that one more, this time a high-up from Sarajevo TV, M.K., has escaped from the city to Pale and joined them. Later on I ring TV Sarajevo to tell them. They're shocked and can't believe it.

I ask the producer M.T. whether with documents from the High Commission for Refugees – saying I work for them – I can go to Sarajevo and 'bring my ill aunt out to Pale'. I have told him and everybody else several times that my son went to England before the war. If they knew he was still in the city, that would be the end of me (and perhaps of him as well).

He tells me: 'Those UN papers mean nothing to the army, which now has total control in Pale. They could kill you on the way, or dress you up in a uniform and send you to the front.'

What to do now?

I listen to Serb leader Radovan Karadžić declaring in Sokolac that they 'know what they want, which is a Serb Republic of Bosnia-Herzegovina', and that they'll 'create it by all means'. According to him, the Croats and Serbs have already divided up the territory and left around 18% for the Muslims.

Old, experienced people say: 'Here a person never knows in which religion or state they'll die.'

Pale, Monday 18 May 1992

I'm writing this on Tuesday, early in the morning.

A woman with a child from Vučja Luka came to our place to phone Sarajevo and find out how her numerous family is faring. They live in all parts of the city, and are married to members of diverse nationalities. Now all that is smashed to smithereens. How can she get accustomed to this, and help all of them when they've now been separated into 'us' and 'them', whereas until recently they'd lived together as a happy family. For forty-seven years we've mingled for love, and now they're dividing us out of hatred. Why do people agree to that?

The two young sisters from Vučja Luka also come to use the phone. They meet my wife and daughter and talk for a long time. I feel better somehow, since I'm no longer entirely alone. They call their boyfriends, chatter on, and arrange what to do so that this Nazi hand does not separate them completely.

They fondle our dogs and tell us about their Oscar, who is a descendant of our older dog Daša.

On Sarajevo TV I watch a column stretching for kilometres, made up of Children's Embassy buses and private cars, as they drive thousands of desperate people away from the burning, bleeding city. It is a journey 'with other stations of hopelessness' – Kafka. Weeping faces of mothers and children can be seen through the windows. Fathers and brothers remain in the city, to fight or to look after apartments. What an apocalyptic splitting of families. All have in common a little hope and a lot of hopelessness.

Perhaps my son too is among them. I know nothing about him. The war caught him in his most dangerous year, the eighteenth. I rely upon his strength and reason to ensure that, in some other world where men are not judged by weapons, he will find himself.

I am rung from Sarajevo – Vojničko Polje by the journalist M.A., who in his flat is hiding two grown young men (his own son and his brother's). Although I know what sort of situation he's in, he jokes about how much boys eat. He goes to the TV building and brings back a bit of food for them from the restaurant. It has been five days now that he has had no water or electricity. If he was alone, he'd have found a way out; as it is, he's protecting them from the hunters of young meat.

Today or tomorrow the tragic predictions about aerial bombardment of Sarajevo may become a reality. I can't believe it.

My God, what will today bring?

S.T., an acquaintance from RTS, calls begging me to help his son, who's a doctor and ran away from Koševo hospital to Pale in his white coat. The young man comes to see us, my wife gives him some clothes to change into. As he eats hungrily, he tells us how in the city he could no longer stand the suspicious looks of patients when they read his name on his coat, and how in Pale they correct him whenever he says Muslim or Croat and tell him he has to say 'ustasha'.

'My profession', he says, 'which knows no nation where a patient is concerned, has been totally degraded.' He is ashamed and doesn't hide it.

He goes off to the Serb hospital in Pale, to see what he'll do. I'm extremely careful with him, since I'm not sure what I can say to him.

I learn that my son didn't join the convoy yesterday, which was halted by SDS soldiers at Ilidža and now the passengers are being held as hostages. They've lodged them in a big sports hall, and negotiations are beginning about the conditions for their release. I've seen this kind of blackmail only in films. The 'negotiations' are being televised and show all the madness and filth of this war.

The young doctor comes just to give us some medicine for Ðulzida. How did he manage to get it, I ask.

'It's an unbelievable madhouse here. Total chaos.' – He smiles bitterly as he leaves.

Two armed soldiers are going round all the Muslim houses, searching them for weapons.

My wife embarks on a general spring cleaning of the house. What's the point of work during a pointless war?

Pale, Tuesday 19 May 1992

6.00 News

Dobrinja, Nedžarići, Vojničko Polje etc. in an agony of hunger and despair. Completely blocked off, without food, water or electricity. There are all of these commodities in Pale, but the Muslims are scared to death since instead of calming down the war is spreading. Only the brave dare go from the Upper Town to the Lower, where all the more important institutions of the Serb regime are located. I think about Dobrinja and Nedžarići and realize that this is the death of New Town and of people's dream that life is easiest in the newer parts of the city.

The Serb leaders propose that Sarajevo be proclaimed an open city for 24 hours, so that people can escape from it with their bare necessities. That is precisely their goal: to empty the city, level it to the ground, ruthlessly kill all its defenders, and then move their own people into the ruins, with the task of rebuilding the city over the next twenty years. All of this then to be celebrated as a great national victory.

I tell myself that this is perhaps a great 'victory' of the Serb army over innocent civilians, but a terrible defeat of the Serb people. Five thousand children and parents are still being held in Ilidža, while the army and the politicians negotiate. I watch those exhausted faces and feel ashamed for being a human being.

Muslims from Sarajevo flee to Croatia, Serbs via Pale to Serbia. Who will populate this city if it remains entirely empty?

B.R. arrives in Pale, the friend in whose house my son is now staying in Sarajevo. Her husband has remained in the city, he refuses to leave their flat or Sarajevo. She's quite frantic, and talks only about the horrors of life in Sarajevo. In her words I sense a reproach for my not having brought my son out to Pale, irrespective of whether they'd then have called him up. She'd save his life, I'd save both his life and his human dignity. Is that possible?

Pale, Wednesday 20 May 1992

Wake up at 4.00. Dawn is breaking. I look out at the garden where onion, parsley, potatoes, celery and currants are growing, and think about how I might send at least a little to our friends in the city. I'm no longer sure that I'll be digging up the potatoes this autumn. I'm no longer sure of anything.

I look through some old newspapers (no papers at all arrive in Pale) and spot an old photograph of Hitler. He looks at me as though he had risen from his grave and was walking round me. He does not need to rise from the dead, his successors are already all about me.

International aid supplies have just arrived in our local shop. This free aid is now being sold by the new authorities to the hungry people. I bought three packets of Dutch margarine, already past its sell-by date. I don't have a penny left. I'm relying on my neighbour Enisa, who has a little shop nearby and gives me food on tick.

Martial law has now been proclaimed in Pale, i.e. the entire civil administration has been suspended. Step by step we are sinking into the darkness of Fascism. They have announced that all those who do not sign a 'declaration of loyalty to the Serb authorities' will be forcibly deported. At the cost of losing my house, my garden and even my life, I'll not sign that.

Nothing, absolutely nothing can force me to put on a uniform and take a gun in my hands. When a person becomes conscious of his position and makes a final decision, he is then altogether calm.

News about the negotiations in Ilidža. 'If you supply the troops in the barracks with food, then we'll let the children leave the city.' The world is gradually discovering the Balkan cast of mind.

Negotiations 'crowned with success'; the exhausted children and mothers are going in a convoy to Split.

An old friend of my mother, N.K., 'reads my fortune in the coffee grounds' and says that everything will be all right and I shouldn't worry. I know she's consoling me, but even that means a lot.

My wife has hung curtains on the windows overlooking the road, even though she'd never liked them. We're not sure whether to laugh at our neighbour, who says: 'If you're hanging curtains, there's bound to be a war, eh!'

Poor Žuža! We now realize why she has been constantly hungry. It's already obvious that she's in pup, even though her belly's still small.

Pale, Thursday 21 May 1992

Nothing, absolutely nothing, just pain and fear.

Pale, Friday 22 May 1992

Negotiations in Lisbon, lull in Sarajevo, martial law in Pale. I'm still under the powerful impression of a TV programme about Fascism. György Konrád says: 'The glass is broken, but you can still drink from it.'

My daughter is beginning to 'go crazy' in Pale. She can't stand it here any longer. She wants to go back to Sarajevo, among people, her friends. Her horror of the people surrounding her in Pale is far greater than her horror of the shells falling on the city. She asks me why they're conscripting everybody into the Serb army when they already have more than enough soldiers. I tell her the army wants to have control over all living souls. Those not under its control are free people, and the army can't tolerate anyone being free. Such people are dangerous.

My editorial colleague the eminent journalist N.A., after nine days spent in prison in SDS-controlled Ilidža, on being set free makes a statement for SRNA that he has been treated correctly. Incredible. To issue such a statement, after nine days in prison without any arrest warrant, trial or right of defence, is astonishing. They even told him to 'leave his flat with his family and go across to the Muslim part of the city'. I know how poor his health is, this will kill him.

What day is it today? Everyone says it's Friday, and I have it down as Thursday: How did I get it mixed up?

It's night. Two strong explosions shake Pale. Meho tells me that 'tonight something's going to happen'. In Renovica (near Pale) two Serb soldiers killed. Revenge is on the way. He's trembling with fear. I try to calm him down, telling him that he and his wife should sleep at our place tonight. Mina comes over too with her daughter and sons, saying that all the Muslims are scared they might be massacred tonight. She talks non-stop to conceal her fear, which irritates me a bit, but I fully understand that fear. Her daughter is calm and says: 'Needless panic'.

My God, what a dark night it is outside. As if everything has died and only death is still alive.

Pale, Saturday 23 May 1992

Our son's birthday. He celebrates it hidden in some cellar, so that the shells can't kill him.

Last night on TV Sarajevo György Konrád recalls his question to György Lukács in Budapest: 'How did you manage to write so many books?' *'Hausarest , Hausarest!'* (house arrest).

During the night I hear the sound of breaking glass near the house. In the morning I discover that the Albanian-owned bakery has been demolished. There's a rumour circulating that two local Serbs did it last night. Total fascism is coming closer and closer.

We've managed to get medicines for our journalist friend P.K. in Sarajevo, who had a kidney transplant a few years ago. Without those medicines he's condemned to a slow death.

My daughter's getting ready to catch a bus to Grbavica and then cross over near Hotel Bristol to the part of the city controlled by the Sarajevo territorial defence forces. She's carrying the medicines and a parcel of food – a dozen eggs, a box of margarine and some vegetables from our garden. My heart aches, since we have so many friends needing help in the city, yet we have so little food apart from salad leaves and onions from the garden. My wife dreams of sending them as much as possible, but my daughter can't carry so much.

This morning we accompany her fearfully to the front door.

I watch a documentary on TV Belgrade which claims that Dubrovnik hasn't been destroyed at all. Only Serb buildings. The lie alone inhabits, exists in these regions. Milk is black and coal is white. What hypocrisy.

Meho comes over to tell us that 'his phone no longer works'. My wife checks. Mina's doesn't work either. We soon learn that all Muslims have had their telephones cut off. Step by step to applied fascism.

'Muslims are dangerous, they can send confidential information to Sarajevo, conspire together and threaten the authorities on the free territory of the Serb Republic of B-H.'

I learn that a young doctor, the son of our closest friends in Pale, telephoned from the States – which he did manage to reach, after many trials and tribulations – to say: 'The former Yugoslavia no longer exists.'

They have shattered the crystal ball here, and now we have only the fragments.

Pale, Sunday 24 May 1992

Dawn breaks. I hear the chirping of birds. I lie in my bed and look at the closed shutters. I hear how life is awakening outside but I don't see it, which reminds me of this almost two-month-long captivity in Pale.

Last night, through a conversation with a close neighbour, I realize how in fact I have no idea about what's really happening around me. A mass of tiny details reveals to me how, with the intensification of repression, revolt and opposition are being born and people are truly discovering themselves.

The young doctor – the son of my colleague from Sarajevo – comes round to say goodbye. He tells me: 'I've seen through it all. I'm going from Pale to Belgrade – I've managed to get some documents – and then out into the world. As far away from all this as possible.'

I'm glad that someone at least will be saved.

A villager called R.J. comes to my garden and weeps as he tells me how ashamed he is that Serb refugees are breaking into weekend cottages near his house. Some are moving in, others are just there to rob. They're carrying off food, furniture, bed linen, clothes. B.R., whose flat in Sarajevo our son is sharing with her husband, in despair tells us the same story. Some people have taken over two weekend cottages, she says, while the ones that have been looted have in some cases been stripped bare, with nothing left but traces of flour, sugar and salt on the floor. They've carried away everything, she says in tears. She went to the local Crisis HQ, but they said there's nothing they can do to stop it. First Muslim weekend cottages, now all those where nobody's living.

I think of how people are accursed beings, and that the curse will follow them to their death.

When I return from the graveyard, I find in our house the husband of my editorial colleague M.J. (the one who was weeping on the phone some ten days ago, asking me somehow to help our arrested friend from Ilidža). He's a professor at the university. He left his wife behind in Grbavica (she didn't want to go), and fled by car to Pale. He is resigned. He needs two litres of petrol to get to his weekend cottage.

I walk round the upper town in search of petrol. I get it from a young man I've never met before. He says: 'I'll give it you because of that film about Dubrovnik.'

I discover that in Pale past and present are in an iron yoke: everything is remembered, everything is known, as if someone had stripped us naked and allowed us to move around our ghetto like that.

On the TV screen I see the selector of the Yugoslav football team, red-eyed, tendering his resignation, because he can't bear to see the destruction of his birthplace and the killing of innocent civilians.

News. The UN High Commission for Refugees has decided to withdraw its people from Sarajevo, for security reasons.

I learn that my colleague N.A. from Ilidža has in fact been exchanged for C., another colleague from *Politika*, who'd been in a Sarajevo gaol. People are being exchanged like merchandise, only with national labels.

'I imagine you like a "porker in Teheran",' I'm told today by S.K., a colleague from the TV who was arrested in Dobrinja by the chetnik side, spent 19 days in prison at Pale and was recently exchanged. The prison, or concentration camp, is some five hundred metres from my house.

A curfew has been imposed on Pale. It's 'as silent as the grave' until daybreak; then you can at least hear the birds.

'A foul word is sweeter than baklava here, and a word deadlier than a bullet', a Bosnian author writes just before he dies.

My wife is watching on Serb TV Ratko Mladić, the new commander they've appointed in place of General Kukanjac. In Croatia they called him 'the butcher from Knin'. He stands on a hill above Sarajevo, bloated with good food, and says: 'I can level it to the ground'.

My wife, appalled, says that Kukanjac is a mere child compared to him.

In Sarajevo there is a shortage of wood for coffins. People are being buried in common graves, in 'open spaces' and parks. All the timber from Pale, from the saw-mill, is transported daily in big trucks to Serbia in exchange for food. If they go on like this, there'll soon be only bare rock round Pale.

It's night, through the window of the house I watch armed men walking slowly along the road. I think that all this is really just a horrible, ugly dream.

Pale, Monday 25 May 1992

Once, so long ago now that I can hardly remember them, celebrations for Youth Day and Tito's birthday. I think about how he missed the chance to move this semi-civilized society slowly towards democracy, and to disburden himself of too much power and authority. Even so there's no denying that in the time of his rule we were at least to some extent 'part of Europe', whereas now we're Europe's slaughter-house.

Until quite recently his picture hung flanked by candles in the apartment of an old friend of my mother's. He had to take it down, because he was scared of his Serb co-nationals, who hate everything Croat.[13]

Our dog Žuža had three puppies this morning: two males and one female. My wife calls them 'Tito's pioneers'. We're happy, because in this world of hatred and death at least something noble is born. How shall we feed them?

They are still shelling Sarajevo. The Holiday Inn, the railway station, the UNIS building...

The people from the hills must be direct descendants of Nero.

---

13.   Josip Broz (Tito) was born in Croatia; his father was Croat and his mother Slovene.

14.30

A thunderbolt. The kind that splits the brain and stops the heart. My daughter gets back from Sarajevo, in a state of shock and in tears, with an enormous black eye.

She tells us how she handed over the medicines to my ill colleague and the food to our friends, and brought away a thousand DM which my friend the radio journalist gave her to take to Pale, for us to forward on to Belgrade for his son the doctor.

Without trouble she passed through the city, crossed the bridge on the Miljacka which divides the two warring sides, and got through the checkpoint at the 'Crisis HQ' in 'Serb Grbavica'; but then somewhere along the way to Pale, in the forests on Jahorina, three bearded young men with cockades stop their minibus. They check the passengers' ID cards, then order out two elderly people and our daughter. Her ID card reveals that she was born in Rijeka. They search all the passengers, and on our daughter they find the marks and take them. She tells them that it's true, then, that the chetniks rob people, at which one of them punches her in the eye. He asks her if she's the daughter of the TV journalist. When she replies in the affirmative, he says: 'That ustasha!'

They go off into the woods with their loot, leaving them alone on the road, since the bus has already driven off. Some military truck picked them up and gave them a lift to Pale.

My daughter draws a sketch of the thug's face on a piece of paper. Perhaps I'll find out one day who the fellow is. How shall I then restrain myself and not become like him?

My wife and I console her, saying that it could have been far, far worse, and we take the decision that tomorrow she'll leave for Belgrade, and then via Hungary and Slovenia to Rijeka.

I can see fear in her eyes, and tears for us staying behind in Pale. She's scared they might kill me. She knows what the words 'that ustasha' mean. I try to persuade my wife to leave too, but she refuses.

'I'll go when I finish my weaving', she jokes.

A sleepless night. I think about my daughter. She's nineteen years old, she has just enrolled at the Architectural Faculty in Sarajevo, and now she has to flee from the place where she grew up. How will she cope on that uncertain journey?

At dawn, with two bags of essential belongings and a big bruise on her face, she leaves for the bus. She fondles our dogs, kisses us, hiding her tears. I tell her: 'This is your world, not theirs.'

'Just don't get sentimental', she replies, and begs us to leave Pale as soon as possible.

I tell her I don't want to run away from our land, from our house. In Sarajevo people are staying to look after their flats, and I'm staying here to look after our home. If I'd left Pale in the first days of the war, I'd have been ashamed of myself till the day I died.

My wife tells me later: 'She has left Bosnia with the very same suitcase I had when I came to Bosnia, almost thirty years ago.'

A night without electricity in Pale reveals to the full how dark the darkness is here.

Of one thing I'm sure: the aggressors and killers in this war are the descendants of the people who were defeated in the last one. I thought their ghost had been buried for good, yet it has now risen from the grave to spread death once more.

Two days ago I watch through my window as they bury our neighbour Hrvo in the nearby Muslim graveyard. He was a hunter and a carpenter. He was on his way to Podvitez (a village just outside Pale, where he was from) when they found a hunting rifle in his car. He was taken to prison and beaten to death. The 'official doctor' diagnosed his death as 'suicide by hanging'. When they buried him naked according to Islamic custom, covered just with a white sheet, they saw that his entire body was covered in bruises.

There are few people at the funeral. Many haven't dared to come, since for the new regime it would be 'showing solidarity with the oppressor'.

Horror outlined by a Pale night.

The words of György Konrád reverberate in my head. But the glass is broken and you can't drink from it any longer.

Pale, Wednesday 27 May 1992

The morning starts off with the news that the maternity hospital has been bombed in Sarajevo. It is a new hospital, built with donations from the citizens. Is any place in Sarajevo 'sacred' to those creatures from the hills?

Another shock for Muslims in Pale. They have been fired from all state-owned enterprises and offices. One more step towards pure applied Fascism.

Even earlier I noticed how Ragib, the manager of my local supermarket, a decent, honest man, had disappeared and all his duties had been taken over by his colleague S., but I didn't pay much attention to it. I thought Ragib was ill. Already in the first days of the war all Muslims were dismissed from the police and the administration. It was all done quietly, 'without any fuss'. The people who experienced it directly didn't say much, fearing something still worse.

Step by step the new authorities in Pale are putting into practice Hitler's idea about the supremacy of one nation over another, about Aryans and Jews. Except it took Hitler a few years to do what these people have done in a few months.

Words are feeble for explaining this, only silence and suffering are left. I don't know if my daughter managed to escape this ghetto. It's a long journey via Romanija, Vlasenica, Zvornik and Serbia to the Hungarian border.

11.00

Horror upon horror.

In the centre of the city, in Vaso Miskin street next to the Market, a shell falls on people queuing for bread. Scores dead and hundreds wounded. A crime to stop your brain from functioning. Who are the people shelling from the hills? Do they know whom they kill, in the name of what aims they kill? They're not human, they're monsters.

I can't look at the chunks of bloody human flesh and shrieks of pain on the screen. I can't breathe, walk, think, I can't stand myself as part of the human race. Is this the summit of the horror, the summit of Golgotha? If there's still more to come, I'd be better off not existing. All that's left for me is wordless silence.

On Serb TV from Pale, my former colleague Rada Đokić says that the Muslims themselves have done this deliberately, the 'green berets' that is, in order to shock the world.[14] I'm beginning to hate my profession from the bottom of my heart. They're not journalists, they're professional killers.

I breathed a little easier when my daughter called from Zagreb. The shadow of the massacre has overlaid my happiness at her escape.

It's night. If sleep comes over me, I'll get at least some relief. A far-off little window shines out over Pale.

I almost forgot. One more argument from Rada Đokić that the whole thing was fabricated: how come that a Sarajevo TV crew was at the scene of the massacre so promptly? Yet she knows very well that a Sarajevo TV post was set up recently in the old radio station, about a hundred metres away, and that mobile crews constantly made the rounds of the city.

Pale, Thursday 28 May 1992

Still under the influence of the massacre in Vaso Miskin street. I can hardly write. All Muslims have had their telephones cut off, they are forbidden to gather in 'public places', even at the bridge near my house where I used to spend happy childhood days.

Muslims have been advised (for now) to leave Pale, in the interest of their own safety. Nobody is driving them out, but...

Where is the 'renowned doctor' Koljević now, who only a month and a half ago was assuring them that nobody was allowed to do anything to them, that his government was democratic and protected the rights of all citizens? Where now is that young,

---

14.   Green berets were worn by SDA militia units, as opposed to regular units of the B-H Army.

ambitious council leader R. Starčević, who grew up in Pale in the company of Muslims? Where now is the spiritual leader of the Serbs Dobrica Ćosić, co-author of the *Memorandum*, who spoke about the creation of a Greater Serbia but without repression or bloodshed?

This is the start of creating pure national territories with unlimited power for national leaders.

I feel as if the circle is tightening round me. My wife warns me to remove from my desk the Catholic prayer book that my late mother left me, and the book I'm reading just now, Rudolf Wiener's *Jesus Christ*.

Yesterday my closest neighbour F. was arrested, today another one, H.

'Don't follow me, I'm lost too' – was written on the rear window of a car driving round devastated Beirut.

This evening not even that little window is lit. Again I hear the muffled thudding of shells being fired from Trebević. How am I supposed to lay my head on the pillow.

The world is shocked by the outrage in Sarajevo.

Pale, Friday 29 May 1992

Walpurgis Night in Sarajevo. General Mladic's orders were : 'ROAST SARAJEVO!'

The city is burning, the dead are no longer counted. Glow from the fires in Sarajevo high in the sky.

The Nero of our time must answer for crimes against humanity.

It's not yet the summit of Golgotha. Along this road there are more and more terrible stations still to come.

Pale, Saturday 30 May 1992

I'm on the brink of total despair because of this continuous muffled noise coming from Trebević.

Over the hedge. Meho says in a trembling voice: 'They'll raze Sarajevo to the ground'.

I flee from hatred, yet with every shell fired it increasingly worms its way into me. From now until death, those killers must be brought to justice.

I play a Johann Sebastian Bach CD very loud, in order to block out all other sounds. I watch the pigeons eating breadcrumbs on the terrace and hear a distant voice: 'We are like pigeons.'

Pale, Sunday 31 May 1992

UN sanctions against Serbia and Montenegro.

A sad, hopeless Sunday.

'Let the dead bury the dead' – *André Gide.*

Pale, Monday 1 June 1992

I cannot think, I cannot write, I cannot live.

Pale, Tuesday 2 June 1992

I cut the grass and clover round the house, and drag it across the road on a handcart to the house of our old friends, who have two cows. In return they bring us milk and cheese.

On the bridge stands a car from which men with black beards and cockades on their fur caps stare at me from bulbous red eyes. They have bandoliers full of bullets across their chests, grenades on their belts, machine pistols in their hands. These are the images of people who I thought belonged only in films, in period reconstructions of times fifty years past. Now they're here, they have swum up from the murky depths of that horrific period and risen from their graves to say they're not dead. To be sure they're just some farmers who have set aside the plough and taken deadly weapons in their hands, in order to mete out their own idea of justice. Here in Pale they're called 'liberators'. The old friend to whom I take the grass says that his 'stomach turned' when he saw them.

There's nobody on the street. The Muslims don't dare to leave their houses. Furtively, when there's no one around, they come over to our place to call their relatives in Sarajevo, Žepče, Zenica. They have given them our phone number, so my wife and I often run over to their houses to fetch them to the phone. I then go out into the garden so as not to disturb them, but I always hear the same story. 'Don't worry, we're all OK, nobody's maltreating us yet, things will get better.' When they finish the conversation, they thank us over and over again. Only in suffering do people become like ants.

Mina comes over with her daughter and little son for a chat. She irritates me a bit because she talks non-stop. When she leaves I feel ashamed, because I know it's only fear talking from her, naked fear for her children. She still has a bit of food stored up.

She'll endure anything – both hunger and fear – so long as her children survive.

The Serb leader Karadžić appeals via SRNA to his generals to stop the artillery bombardment of towns. What cynicism.

I learn that a former friend from Pale has been promoted to command the units which from Trebević are shelling people – our friends in Sarajevo – with whom two years ago he celebrated New Year's Eve in my house. I can hardly wait to look him in the eye again. I think about him coming to arrest me.

That diminutive girl from SA-3 (TV Sarajevo, Channel 3) came over yesterday, and after a telephone conversation with her boyfriend she says she has to go to the city, be with him and work for TV Sarajevo.

I think of how much decency and courage there is in that delicate little body, and how much slime and evil in those 'great men' who have led their armed herds out onto Trebević.

The dogs are forever barking, since more and more strangers – mostly women, some younger some older – pass up or down the road in search of 'houses to exchange'. A refugee woman from Vogošća has moved into my sister's flat. We expected anyway that someone would move in. Better a woman with children than armed, drunken 'liberators'.

Pale, Wednesday 3 June 1992

Another shock. My colleague and good friend K.J., now one of the main editors, calls to tell me that S.T, the journalist from SA-3, will be arrested if she comes to Sarajevo. He tells me it's because of her parents who are in Vučja Luka, and in whose Sarajevo flat 'something compromising' has been found. I can't believe it. What has the girl hidden? They can't reject and condemn *her* because of her parents. She refused to work for SRNA – what else does she have to do to prove her loyalty?

'Why did she leave the city?', the editor asks curtly.

Another shock. An acquaintance of mine from the TV, M.J, who was forever accusing and threatening me because some six or seven years ago I'd made a documentary in Kosovo about the isolation of the Albanians, goes past our house accompanied by an armed soldier. He has never forgotten me. And now he has come to Pale. What is he going to do? Now he can do anything.

When I'm overcome by despair, I carry on with making a tall wooden fence round my house. It's no longer just an aesthetic matter.

Pale, Thursday 4 June 1992

I lie in my room and listen to the monster of war breathing all round me.

Pale, Friday 5 June 1992

A sleepless night. Around midnight volleys of automatic fire at Muslim houses begin. These are all our neighbours and friends. There's a lot, all kinds of things, that we haven't had in life, but of friends we've always had plenty.

My daughter used to describe to me how in Sarajevo gunfire doesn't cause all that much fear, because everyone knows it's the people up there on the hills. Here in Pale it insinuates itself into your very bones, it paralyses your brain, it's so close you can almost touch it with your hand. Nobody knows what happens in the darkness, nobody dares to go out onto the street, we're all driven into our dark rooms where we count the hours until daybreak. Night-time here is like the crater of a reawakened volcano. A person is totally alone, left to the tender mercies of the barbarians.

In the morning I look at the scared, lost faces of our Muslim neighbours, as they wander aimlessly round their gardens, not daring to go out onto the street. To the local regime Pale is free territory, where democracy, freedom and prosperity reign.

On TV I watch pictures of one of the decisive days in Sarajevo – the evacuation of the big Marshal Tito barracks. A long time ago, when it was built, it was situated on the periphery of Sarajevo, now it's right in the centre of town. It divides the new from the old part of the city. If the Serbs capture it, they'll cut the city in two and certainly take the new part all the way to Ilidža. I learn that last night local Serbs riddled with bullets the house of Beka, a barber from the Upper Town. That young man, a friend of mine, had never harmed anyone.

The evacuation of the barracks is proceeding 'according to plan'. The army is leaving it with reluctance. I watch a comic scene on TV, with some Sarajevo territorial troops pushing the car of a JNA officer – a musician. 'Now to exterminate the rats on Trebević', a cheerful territorial says into the camera.

In the afternoon all connections severed with Croatia and Slovenia. I fight against panic and despair, since this is my only 'exit to the world'.

The TV reception has been very bad since Hum was bombarded. However, we have the pleasure of choosing between three Serb channels, which owe their excellent reception to stolen relays.

We get a visit from the wife of M.R., who's now shelling Sarajevo from Trebević. She's wearing black.. Her mother died in Vojkovići, near Ilidža. She has spent most of her life in Sarajevo, worked there up until the war, yet neither for one moment nor with one word does she express any sorrow for that city and the people in it. She says: 'The system's to blame for all this, it's all orchestrated by the Vatican, the people aren't to blame.' My wife restrains herself and merely says: 'There's no system that would make me kill anybody. I'll die without ever understanding all this hatred.'

She asks about our children, and as usual we pretend that they're in England.

'Wise, very wise', she keeps repeating. I wonder if she'd feel at all sorry if she knew they'd been – and my son still was – in Sarajevo.

'Forget Sarajevo. It's a dead city. It no longer exists. There's no life there any more', she repeats for the umpteenth time, and asks my wife if it's true that people are dying of hunger in the city. My wife can't resist answering that she has herself witnessed how the citizens of Sarajevo are in fact simply all on a big macrobiotic diet and cleansing of the organism through hunger treatment; and how this has simply strengthened them, so that they radiate the most unbelievable optimism.

She tells us how her husband said: ' Just so long as I don't get blood on my hands!' As if firing shells at Sarajevo doesn't mean getting blood on your hands. How people do try to run away from the truth.

How close we once were, and how far apart now. I feel sick at the thought of the days I spent with him. It was all lies and deceit. What would our mutual friend Ešef (Keša) have said to all this – who was lucky enough to leave for a job in Libya back in January?

Night falls over Pale. The wife of our former friend goes out into her world, we remain alone and wait in trepidation for the nightly volleys of gunfire.

Pale, Saturday 6 June 1992

Night, 2.00

How can I lay my head on the pillow when through it I can hear what's happening in Sarajevo? I have no cigarettes or alcohol to calm me down at least a little. I have only this noise that goes right through me.

When day breaks I learn from my neighbour that yesterday at Žepa near Rogatica some Serb soldiers, most of them from Pale, were ambushed by the 'berets'. Dozens dead, many more wounded. Among them was my former teacher's son, whom they'd forcibly conscripted. The young man loved music, and hated the army. He gave his life for the 'great patriotic cause'. My God, what a nightmare.

Pale is covered with casualty notices, on which is written: 'slain by fiendish Muslim hands'. The young man who died at Žepa had so many Muslim friends in Pale. They've now been gripped by panic and fear, and some Muslims are now fleeing by roundabout paths to relatives in Podvitez – a village near Pale.

Tonight vengeance is being prepared, vengeance upon the Muslims. They'll let loose the armed chetniks, like dogs from the leash, to kill the terrified people. You can almost touch the fear with your hand and feel it with all your senses.

Mina arrives in an agitated state to ask if she and the children can sleep at our place tonight. Meho asks the same thing. The doors of our house are always open to them, yet I wonder how I can protect them?

Mina tells me in the evening, when she arrives with her daughter and son: 'Who is not with them is against them, so even you can't provide me with security, but it's still better with you than alone in our house.' They're hoping their elder son has managed to escape across some fields to Podvitez; her husband will sleep at a Serb friend's house.

'If we're separated, perhaps someone may survive', she says. They've also brought a little dog with them, their daughter's pet.

How long and terrible will this night be? I believe, I hope, like a drowning man clutching at a straw, that nothing will happen, but people can feel in their bones that ANYTHING may happen.

I watch the armed soldiers through the window, walking in twos round the upper town 'to protect the Muslims from Serb soldiers who are out of control'.

I go over to my mother's house and leave a coin before the image of Our Lady, for the salvation of us all. I'm quite aware that if a massacre starts we'll be finished too.

A sleepless night. Registering every sound, senses painfully on edge. Mina and her two children sleep. Is she sleeping? She talked non-stop all evening to dispel her fear, but fear is like water, it fills every crevice and finds new outlets.

Pale, Sunday 7 June 1992

I greet the morning awake, with my head and eyes aching terribly. I stagger round the house, glad that the dogs haven't barked at anyone's steps on the gravel path to our house. Nothing has happened, everything's fine, I tell myself as I peer through the curtains on our windows. My wife always hated curtains, and put them up only a fortnight ago. It feels odd in the morning until we open the shutters. Both my wife and I like a lot of light in the house, and as little darkness as possible.

'Sarajevo is looking more and more like Vukovar', says a reporter on the 6.00 news. Mina and her children leave the house separately to avoid suspicion. They'll come back again tonight.

I go to visit my mother's grave, aware that it's becoming highly dangerous. On the road by the graveyard two armed men stop and stare at me. What's going on in their heads? They can call me over and say: 'Come with us'.

What cycle of crime is forever being repeated on this accursed piece of the earth's crust? People haven't drawn any lessons at all from the past.

'Do not kill, though you be killed', it says in the Talmud, while Rommel fifteen minutes before drinking cyanide tells his son: 'You must never be a soldier.'

A sunny Sunday afternoon. My wife brings me one of the puppies over to the garden table and says: 'To make you feel a bit better!'

The guns can still be heard from the direction of Sarajevo. Helicopters fly continuously over Pale. When will the fuel run out, and this monstrous war machine grind to a halt and become a junk heap of old metal? When?

Meho walks round his garden, completely lost. He has made some wooden shutters for his ground-floor windows, he keeps locking doors, he comes to my garden and talks to me for a long time, searching for an answer to the fateful question of what's to become of them. Armed men have already come to his house asking about his son, who went to work in America a couple of years back.

Pale, Monday 8 June 1999

Last night I heard a huge explosion not far from Pale. Different from previous ones. The windows and walls shook. I learn that last night the first shells fell on Derventa near Pale. People are now talking only about this, whispering. 'Will Pale meet the fate of Sarajevo?' I'd like that, for people to feel at least a little of the horror that for months has shaken Sarajevo, even if the first shell were to fall on my house.

From my garden I look across the Miljacka to Imet's big house, where Dr. Šućur, a doctor from the hospital in Koran, has recently moved in. Not knowing this, two other Serb reservists broke into it this morning, and now they're quarrelling about who it belongs to, with submachine-guns in their hands! This morning my neighbour Fadil, who built and opened the Old Bridge restaurant bar a few months ago, told me that all the Muslims in Pale and the surrounding villages have been ordered to leave. I cannot believe it. I keep telling him it's just a rumour. His eyes are red from lack of sleep. His restaurant has been closed for a long while. He brings me a bottle of cognac and says: 'It's better you drink it than them.'

My wife is looking through our family photos, picking the ones to take with us. We instinctively feel that the moment of departure is drawing closer.

Today is the funeral of the slain young men from Pale. As 15.00 draws closer, the hour of the funeral, panic rises among the Muslims. One of them asks me: 'What is this, are we all going to be massacred?'

I tell him it's not true, that the Muslims of Pale have nothing to do with politics, but fear of imminent death or exile is mirrored in his eyes. What if that actually does happen?

My brain is no use any more, it only deceives me. Today only animal instincts matter.

It's noon, there's no electricity. They call me from the TV to say that the Sarajevo territorial forces have decided to 'go for broke'. They've taken Mojmilo, Dobrinja is in flames, they're getting closer to Vraca, to the Jewish Cemetery. Hundreds have died.

How about my son? If he can just stay alive and remain sane. Perhaps this is the culmination of it all, perhaps, but I doubt it, perhaps it's just the beginning of the real war.

Since the first shells fell on Pale, people have been wandering round the concrete cellars of the houses, thinking about how to protect themselves. When I was building my house with lots of windows and glass doors a few years ago, the builder Marko told me it was obvious I hadn't experienced a real war. His own house is like a concrete fortress.

I go out into the street, and some armed fellow yells: 'Halt, come here!' 'Who, me?', I ask. Another armed whipper-snapper recognizes me and tells him: 'No, not him.' It won't be long before we need a pass for our garden or the street.

My neighbour Miralem asks me tearfully what he should do, because they've been told they have to move out, as their safety cannot be 'guaranteed' any longer.

The funeral of the Serb soldiers, broadcast on Pale TV, is transformed into a kind of political rally. With all the leaders present, their youth and their death is being used for the purpose of 'realizing the historic goals of the Serb people'. I'm quite certain this lot are absolutely not representatives of the Serb people, perhaps of one extreme, militant part of it, but what does that matter when other, normal Serbs have mutely gone over to them. They're creatures of Hitler and Stalin, psychopaths.

'After the funeral, they boarded a helicopter for Belgrade', an acquaintance of mine informs me. Will this people ever open its eyes and realize that it's being led to destruction like a flock of sheep?

In the evening, separately, Mina and her children come over to spend the night. They bring a bit of coffee and food. Her fifteen-year-old daughter is still maintaining that it's all 'needless panic'. Our marriage witness M. tells us her house too is full of 'guests'.

23.00

The thunder of guns from the direction of Sarajevo has stopped — what does it mean?

Pale, Tuesday 9 June 1992

1.00, 2.00, 3.00, 4.00, 5.00. Dawn breaks. Silence. Does this presage peace or some still greater nightmare? Through the half-open window I watch soldiers marching up and down the street. Later on I learn that they've been deployed to the surrounding meadows and woods. They've blocked all exits from this part of Pale, inhabited by Muslims, a few Serbs, and the two of us who are nothing, just ordinary human beings, to whom national identity is the most unimportant thing in the world.

It is true, a dreadful truth that takes your breath away. They're making lists of Muslims, who have to abandon their homes, land and livestock, and leave in a convoy for Sarajevo, Olovo or

Kladanj. Lucifer himself couldn't have devised a worse punishment for these people. Despair, grief and poverty. The new regime reveals its true face, fully and without prevarication.

I learn that the American Sixth Fleet has been placed on a state of alert. People are saying that Pale too is on the list of possible targets.

Some Italian journalists, who were bringing me money so that I'd have something to live off in Pale, were stopped at Zvornik by the chetniks, who threatened to put a bomb under their car if they proceeded further. They had papers in order from the SDS branch in Belgrade.

There's no electricity and I'm baking bread in my mother's old oven. She always told me not to throw it away, because it might be needed. I thank God that after surviving two wars she didn't live to see this third one, worse and dirtier than all those before it. I've learnt how bread is made when you don't have any yeast.

The sky has cleared, the thunder has stopped, but now I hear the guns again.

In the afternoon S.T, the SA-3 journalist, comes over and I give her the message from the Television. She takes it calmly, saying the important thing for her is that her boyfriend in Sarajevo knows it's not true what they're saying about her parents. She has to get to the bottom of it and clear her name.

Meho's wife Đulzida can't leave the house any more. She's a brave woman, but she tells my wife: 'Meho won't let me, ever since I told him how some soldiers threatened me from a car, pointing at my *dimije*. If the truth be known I only wear them out of superstition, because once long ago I had a dream in which I was told that if I took them off some harm would befall my son.'

Pale, Wednesday 10 June 92

I'm lying in the garden, on a wooden bench, while rain falls on me. I remember the song: 'Raindrops on my forehead'. I can't move. I feel how the plague is laying waste this poor country, on which shells and raindrops fall. They bring death and life.

In Pale, more and more women in mourning and death notices on the telegraph poles.

All telephone links with Sarajevo cut off. I have no news of my son or my friends.

As soon as it gets dark in Pale, no one is allowed to leave their house any more apart from soldiers and true Serbs .

Like a mole in its burrow, I try to decipher the intensity of the plague around me.

An advance contingent of UNPROFOR has arrived in Sarajevo to open the airport. Attacked in Lukavica, one officer is wounded. Is this the beginning of salvation for the people of Sarajevo?

Mina and her children are no longer sleeping with us. She says she has calmed down a little.

Pale, Thursday 11 June 1992

'May God grant they dance on your grave', says the journalist M.P in his commentary — who at first was totally pro-Serb, then somehow detached himself from them, and from the first days of the war threw in his lot with our people from TV Sarajevo. Whatever happened to him, for him to change sides?

This morning a notice made its appearance on the gates to the Pale sawmill: 'Entry prohibited for all NON-SERBS'.

Another step towards pure fascism.

Noon. A van stops in front of the house and eight men armed to the teeth climb out. I was in my garden chopping wood.

In a rough tone of command they ask me to open up my mother's old house, so that they can carry out a search. No warrant, no explanation. They keep their fingers on their submachine-gun triggers. Milanka, a refugee from Vogošća, and her two children live on the second floor.

I climb up the narrow concrete stairs. They take up position in front of the house, at ground-floor level and on the stairs. I beg them not to frighten this woman and her young children. Their leader thrusts me aside at the entrance and bursts into the flat. The woman is trembling with fear, the little girl is crying. They ask her who she is, and what she is. They search the bedrooms, turn everything upside down – furniture, mattresses, stove, chimney, everywhere. They behave like lords of heaven and earth, life and death.

'Now the bottom flat', their commander orders.

'There's nobody down below, it was my late mother's flat', I tell him as I go down the stairs.

'Lucky my mother's not alive', I think once more, as I watch them rummaging through her things with their dirty hands. She wouldn't have survived this. They go into her bedroom, where there's a figure of Our Lady in a carved wooden frame, which my mother brought back from Lourdes in 1935.

They question me about my nationality and my parents' religion. I reply.

'What did your father do?'

'Until 1940 he owned a hotel on Jahorina, and then in 1963 he hanged himself, when they confiscated his land in Pale.

He looked at me as he would at a mangy dog, then began to sift through the coins round the statue (gifts for the Church).

I recognized the youngest among them. He was not even twenty, and I remember that in the past he always used to greet me politely. Now he looked mutely at the floor, with his submachine-gun propped against his leg.

They also searched the ground floor and the garage. We went out into the garden. I saw curtains twitching on nearby windows.

'Please, what's this all about?', I asked.

'We received a report that armed Muslims were hiding in this house', the commander said.

'They do come here, but just for coffee.'

'You don't drink coffee with butchers', one of them yells. They left.

M. brought me some milk and said she'd nearly fainted when she saw armed men round the house.

I'm still in a state of shock. I can't shake it off. Was this search an overture for something worse? I must warn Mina to be on her guard.

Today is Kurban Bajram. Sarajevo is still being shelled.

Mina's daughter comes round, in tears because they have to go off to Sarajevo. She keeps repeating: 'Like Jews! Is it my fault I'm a Muslim?' She's also weeping because she has to leave her pet dog. My wife weeps with her. I go into the bedroom, to avoid watching.

Serbia is beginning to totter. The news programme on Belgrade TV irresistibly recalls the news bulletins from Romania before the fall of Ceauşescu. Telegrams of support for the 'Butcher of the Balkans' , as one American paper has dubbed Milošević, arrive by the thousand.

The Serbs have not deserved to be led by a banker and a psychiatrist [Milošević and Karadžić] down the road to crime and ruin.

What will this night be like? It's raining. Not a single window lit in the surrounding houses.

On account of the insane idea of ethnically pure territories, tomorrow a certain number of Muslims must leave Pale.

Pale, Friday 12 June 1992

The morning when, three years ago, my mother died. According to her wish, I buried her in the Catholic graveyard, in their family grave.

My father was buried in the Orthodox one. I said to myself back then: 'Let them bury me here too, next to her.' I thank God she didn't live to see this terrible day, when her Muslim neighbours, with whom she shared good and ill throughout her entire life, are crying like little children because they have to abandon their homes, their land, their cows and sheep, and set off bundle in hand for a refugee hell. They stand in the road near our house, and like felled trees wait for the buses to pick them up and ferry them away. One of Fascism's most terrible features is the way it uproots people and turns them into meaningless numbers.

Mina's daughter, her dog in her arms, rushes across to tell us quickly that they're staying here after all. Her eyes shine with happiness. Old Meho embraces me, and says through his tears: 'Let them cut my throat, but I'm not going anywhere.'

Of one thing I'm certain: the harm that the new Serb authorities in Pale are doing to these people will one day rebound on them.

My son's friend S., who is the same age as him (18 years old), lost a leg on Trebević, the doctors are fighting to save the other one. A nightmare. My wife has been crying all day. Do the generals of the Serb army know, does it matter to them in the least, that a forcibly conscripted young man became a cripple on Trebević while firing shells at his comrade in the city?

What punishment can be devised for such monsters? They absolutely must stand trial for war crimes against their own and other peoples.

The column of buses with the Muslims has returned to Pale. They couldn't get through to Sarajevo, because some chetnik – 'who along with his troop had become a renegade from the legal authorities' – threatens to massacre the lot of them, up in the hills.

At the bus station, a throng of women and children with bags and bundles are in flight to Serbia. Serb refugees roam about the upper town, wondering which are Muslim houses. Some of them do look genuinely tragic, but there are not a few whose villainy literally stares you in the face.

Pale, Friday 13 June 1992

I light a candle on my mother's grave. In the garden of a nearby house, women in black are setting out tables. That's where our acquaintance R.J. lives, the craftsman who made the tombstone. He lost his only son in Žepa a week ago. Some people say it's God's punishment on the father, who protected the nearby weekend cottages from being broken into by Serb refugees, but himself surreptitiously removed food and other things from them. He looked an honest man, and perhaps this story isn't true. The only truth is that he no longer has a son.

The famous leader and psychiatrist holds a press conference in Belgrade, and announces a cease-fire over the city from Monday. He's no ordinary liar, he's an ontological liar, his whole being is built on lies.

I hear a report on the radio that: 'Sarajevo stinks of burning and faeces. There's fear of epidemic.'

I feel somewhat easier: they rang to let me know they'd seen my son. 'He doesn't say much, like you, but he looks well.'

I'm relying on the promise of B.K. from the Jewish Community to get him out in the first group that leaves the city by plane.

Today's a holiday in our house. After two months, I've finally tasted a piece of roast meat. Yesterday a friend from Pale who hasn't changed lent me 100 German marks. We can live for another month.

Evening falls over Pale. The thud of cannon and multiple rocket launchers reaches us from Trebević. A full, red moon rises above the horizon.

The psychiatrist and his vampires continue to lead the dance of death. They have the 'honour' to have created the largest concentration camp in the history of humanity – Sarajevo. I'm confident that the people of Sarajevo will endure all their experiments.

If these war criminals are ever brought to trial, I shall be a witness from Pale, this 'heart of darkness'.

Another night without electricity. I lie in my bed and think about days spent in Sarajevo, friends and love, a faraway forest and a meadow where I lay on the grass.

I feel somehow that my life hasn't become just a past, that a future exists too.

Those vampires have neither. That's why they destroy and kill. They won't for long. The penalty must be paid.

Pale, Sunday 14 June 1992

It's two hours after midnight. Rain is falling. The rain means salvation for Sarajevo: it will clean the sewers, wash away the filth and blood from the streets. It will never be able to wash it from the faces and hands of the murderers from Trebević.

The telephones are working again. An acquaintance from the Television tells me that from Monday the airport will start to be reopened. Is this the beginning of salvation, or one more trick?

Has the ontological liar decided to trick even himself and carry out the provisions of the agreement?

It's cold. I've lit a fire in the grate and think about the poor wretches in the city, burning their parquet flooring in order to keep warm or cook. In less than two months of war they've been forced back hundreds of years, to the time of the cavemen.

For the third night running there's no electricity. Outside you can hear only the barking of abandoned dogs, who now wander around vainly searching for their owners, and the occasional gunshot or burst of firing. Are the wild passions of the killers calming down, or is it a lull before still fiercer ones erupt?

Yesterday S. told me how she watched people, prisoners, being loaded onto trucks in front of the central prison in Pale. One woman, until then a peaceable housewife, shrieks: 'Slaughter the vermin, why are you sparing them?'

Perhaps women are worse than men.

My editorial colleague M.J., once a great teetotaler and moral purist, rang this morning and told me that she'd found six bottles of *lozovača* at her neighbour's place, and that every day as she languishes in the company of an ailing mother in her Grbavica flat, she drinks one of them. I congratulate her for having finally become a real human being, with the appropriate vices and virtues.

I can't listen to the news on TV and radio, so I don't know what's happening 'in the world', whether it has decided to save us or unconcernedly let us die in this prison.

The Muslims have lost all hope of staying in Pale; now they're just saving their skins.

Pale, Monday 15 June 1992

In Belgrade a general strike by students has begun, demanding the removal from power of Slobodan Milošević. In Sarajevo French specialists are examining the airport runway. They've rung to say that today's Sarajevo *Večernje novine* has reported, under the headline 'Shells Fall on Pale', that because of my refusal to work for 'the Nazi-fascist Television of the Serb Republic of B-H, I'm being maltreated and persecuted here'. I now expect them to come for me, and forcibly seat me in front of a camera to 'deny these lies'. Not for anything in the world will I appear on their television. The first day of the cease-fire signed in Sarajevo has 'by and large' been respected, though there still are snipers and shells. The actor Nermin Tulić, whom I know, lost both legs when a shell exploded outside the Café Sirano. His life is no longer in danger.

There's a hope that the first plane evacuating children from Sarajevo may leave in five or six days.

My wife is sharing with friends in Pale the salad that she'd been growing all this time for friends in the city. Our garden has never been more beautiful and fruitful.

What will this night bring? False hope or real disaster?

Pale, Tuesday 16 June 1992

What relief and joy. After a long while spoke to my son. As soon as the airport is back in service, he'll go far away from this slaughterhouse, a thousand miles away from this darkness. My daughter is waiting in Rijeka for papers to go to England. This war has broken us into pieces that will be difficult to put together again.

I watch how, from the storage tank standing in front of Imet's big house, with its compartments full of petrol that he purchased in earlier days for his own needs, municipal utility workers are siphoning off and stealing the fuel. Yesterday they broke into a nearby workshop – a repair centre for power saws owned by Nezir, a taxi-driver from Sarajevo – and carried off all the very expensive machinery. Stealing cars from Muslims has become a 'national sport' among armed Serbs. People look at it as something 'quite normal'. Actually they know very well what it is, but nobody dares say anything.

Rešo, the owner of a small shop selling cigarettes and fruit, has been ordered to close it down. Next door to him there's a Serb shop that continues to work normally – only the choice of goods is poor. Rešo is already getting ready to abandon everything and leave on a convoy bound for Sarajevo.

Pale, Wednesday 17 June 1992

A day like a dream. With half a kilo of minced meat, *japrak* (wild vine leaves) from our garden, a beef bone, a little cheese, home-baked bread and lots of salad we've made lunch for eight of our old friends. Even the two sisters from Vučja Luka came. I look at the people sitting round me at table, and I see only lost, damaged people without their nearest and dearest. In spite of the minimal food, nobody went hungry; we were happy to feel like human beings again, in a world that recognizes the existence only of national beings. For a long while I cannot sleep out of happiness and a certain new hope that has entered our house.

Pale, Thursday 18 June 1992

Our good fortune continues. My breath was taken away this afternoon when Đ.M., an acquaintance of mine from Koper [Slovenia], knocked on my door together with some Italian journalist. They'd got through to Pale via Zvornik and brought me 500 German marks from a friend in Slovenia. Real wealth in our present circumstances. I invite them to stay with us, but they say they've already booked in to a bed and breakfast in Pale.

I thank God and my friends from Koper for the money, but am now a little worried about these people, since if they're being welcomed warmly by the director of Serb Television in Pale then I'm not sure what to make of them. My God, what a lot has happened yesterday and today. After six days of darkness, the electricity too – light! – has come on. What joy.

Pale, Friday 19 June 1992

It's the easiest thing to recognize fools here – they're the ones who believe in the latest cease-fire agreement.

Last night, today, the merciless bombardment of Sarajevo goes on. Street battles in the city. At the public health institute (near the flat where my son is now), two people killed by a shell.

Today an agreement was signed for monitoring the heavy weapons round the airport, a first step towards getting it back into operation. Another trick, or a thread of hope for the starving people?

In Pale, they're driving away truck-loads of goods stolen from Muslim shops. 'Everything must be taken from the foe.'

News: in Dobrinja and Nedžarići, where we too once lived, the chetniks cut the throats of some fifteen people. I can't believe it, but anything is now possible. Crime has become our everyday reality.

Pale, Saturday 20 June 1992

Last night I'm again unable to sleep. The big guns never stop unloading their deadly burden on the city. As though they want to kill and destroy as much as possible before today's cease-fire comes into force at 11.00.

I lie in my garden and look at the green strawberries just beginning to turn red, and with tears in my eyes I remember a meadow where I ate some last year. Shall I ever go there again? I'll soon be fifty. They say that's the most critical period for a man. I feel as if I can leave all this which we've created over the years and begin again from the beginning. I have to!

16.00 News.

Shock. All activities to do with re-opening the airport are being halted for 48 hours, until fighting stops.

I learn that an exchange in kind of prisoners is taking place: a woman is worth 40 bullets, a man an automatic rifle or a machine gun.

Report that Trebinje is being shelled. When I was in the devastated Dubrovnik in January '92, people told me: 'Trebinje will pay, from here to eternity!' Now the Serbs are calling upon the world to condemn 'this demented killing of civilians'.

The B-H Presidency has announced a general mobilization and the introduction of labour duties for everyone. What does that mean for my son, who has just turned eighteen? At the time of the elections, when all these politicians came to power, he didn't even have the right to vote.

Tonight Mozart must be louder than the familiar sounds from the hills.

Pale, Sunday 21 June 1992

A sunny, warm, blossoming, accursed, sad Sunday in Pale. The bells of the Orthodox church are tolling. Another young life has ceased to exist. The leaders need yet more young, strong flesh to achieve their pathological goals.

One woman, the mother of twins who were killed on the same day in Žepa, took two pistols and set off in search of Karadžić, to kill him. But the doctor is well protected. The salesgirl from a nearby shop, a close relative of the slain twins, sits behind the counter in mourning and simply holds her tongue. It was mainly Muslims who used to visit that shop, make their purchases and gossip about local happenings. Now they've disappeared. With their bags packed, they're waiting to be summoned to the convoy. We've completely lost track of one of our best friends, J.O., who as a Serb felt under threat in Hrasno (held by the Sarajevo territorial units), so he fled to a friend's abandoned flat in Grbavica, held by the Serbs. According to one version, he was sent to forced labour in Lukavica, according to another the Serbs gave him a weapon and thrust him into the front line, while according to a third version he's already dead. His wife is already in Belgrade and I'm afraid to tell her anything.

Some mutual friends who have moved into his flat in Hrasno tell us that, while he was there, nobody troubled him. Strange. Why did he feel threatened, why did he move to Grbavica, held by people of his nationality? Herein perhaps lies also the answer to all questions.

Pale, Monday 22 June 1992

Nightmare. I can't bear to think of it. A shell landed in Tito street, near the National Bank, killing nine people and wounding sixty.

I wander round the house and garden like a blind man, while images of bloody bodies revolve in my mind. My neighbour Meho comes, taking care that no one will see him, and phones his daughter in Sarajevo: 'Everything's fine, don't worry about a thing.'

I look at him and see a wholly changed person. He's now an old man whose voice and hands tremble, whose eyes have lost their shine, while disjointed words pour from him.

Midnight. News. Not nine but nineteen dead, not sixty but a hundred wounded. Today is the longest day in the year and the shortest night.

Pale, Tuesday 23 June 1992

I can't get to sleep because of the terrible images from Tito street, and the report by Rada Đokić, a former colleague from the Television. She's now saying for Belgrade TV that: 'the green berets deliberately placed a pressure-activated mine so that civilians would die and provoke a reaction from world public opinion.'

I can no longer plumb the depths of journalistic lying and perversion. I think that some, almost all, journalists are the worst kind of people, rising to the surface of this criminal war.

Our former neighbourhood of Nedžarići, where we spent eight years, taken and destroyed by the chetniks. About one hundred women and children, in a long column, crossed the bridge over the Miljacka and are now sleeping in the halls of the B-H Parliament.

I swing between despair to my left side and despair to my right. They hold me in their grip and don't relax for a moment.

My wife calls up numerous friends in Sarajevo. There are more and more telephones that nobody answers.

Pale, Wednesday 24 June 1992

Today is my fiftieth birthday. They have passed by like childhood, like a dream.

Once I used to think about things, was close to suicide because of the metaphysical meaninglessness of everything, including my own existence. Now I think about how to survive – that's meaning.

Late last night the barking of the dogs in the house heralds uninvited quests. It's M.T., the producer from Serb TV, who knows we're stuck, that he can come at any time of day or night as if to his own house, since this is now their territory, their rule. He's drunk. With him is a cameraman, G., who I discover only now has left his colleagues at TV Sarajevo and gone over to Pale.

They're armed with pistols and grenades. They toy with them on the table. The producer is surprised they haven't taken me away already. He starts accusing me again, and cannot understand my reasons for refusing to work for SRNA. At the same time he explodes with anger against certain 'Serb journalists' who've remained in Sarajevo.

'I'd kill the lot in one go', he tells me. I tell him that many of his colleagues who've come to Pale have done so purely out of self-interest. To get rich quick and grab some power. He flares up at these words and talks with disgust about Serb soldiers who are 'losing their lives on Pero Kosorić square merely because their hands are full of looted goods'. He speaks scornfully of his colleagues in Pale, who used to fawn on the communist leaders and now fawn on the Serb ones. He was a talented producer for

Sarajevo TV, but now he has signed up heart and soul to restoration of the Serbian Empire. A strange combination of visionary and dangerous, sinister man who could easily kill. He 'respects the ustashe, because they're more professional than the chetniks, who are not even a pale shadow of the former, true chetniks'.

I turn to ice when they tell me the well known TV writer and producer S.S., at whose house our friend J.O. from Hrasno has been hiding lately, was killed in Grbavica.

M.T. says an incredible thing – that now even he feels sorry for 'the Turks', so many of them have been killed and driven from their homes by the Serbs.

When I first met him I was a bit scared, because he can do anything he likes to me. That fear has now subsided, melted away, after two months of isolation in Pale.

His baby-faced friend tries to persuade him they should leave, since it's late. Even he's afraid of the people in Pale. He never knew they were 'so screwed up'.

The producer has had no children from his marriage, nor has his marriage been a happy one, and in these moments he seems almost to be wishing he lived like us. I don't know, perhaps I'm wrong, but it was after midnight when he finally tore himself away.

I take a deep breath. As if all night I'd been walking a tightrope stretched over an abyss. To tell him what I think is tantamount to suicide, not to say anything is tantamount to the most abject cowardice. These things look much simpler on the screen.

My wife tells me it was easier for her to bear almost a month of shelling in Sarajevo than this man's visit and conversation.

There you're with your own people, who warm you with their love and concern, but here we're completely alone, surrounded by these people from whose eyes death stares.

I listen on the radio to the statement of one of the Serb leaders: 'Whoever is a-national today has passed sentence on himself.'

Pale, Thursday 25 June 1992

Telephone conversation with a friend in Sarajevo, who says that 'military intervention will follow within the next few days'. In Sarajevo they're relying on it more and more, yet I'm utterly sceptical. No one is going to want to plunge into the Balkan cauldron, of that I'm sure.

Through people we know in Belgrade, we try to find out how you can get from Serbia into Hungary. My wife sorts through our clothes and things daily, tidies the cupboards, and considers what's most important to take with us.

When our daughter was leaving, she begged us too to go at once. My wife said jokingly: 'We shall, as soon as I finish my weaving.' Now she sits in her room and weaves. She goes out into the garden more and more rarely.

In an educational programme on Serb radio they call the Serbs 'Christ-like'. There's a limit to everything, except stupidity.

I stroke my dog and say: 'We'll see each other again one day'.

I watch our neighbour Fadil, the café owner, transporting boxes of drink on a tarpaulin-covered handcart from the closed café to a little shed near our house. He's still hoping he won't have to leave. The Muslims who have lost that hope have their bags and bundles already packed.

Pale, Friday 26 June 1992

I'm increasingly filled with a quiet despair. Last night another nocturnal visit. This time by our former friend from Pale M.R. with his wife, and our common acquaintance M.J. who left Sarajevo a few days ago. His wife remained in Sarajevo and is still working for the Television.

Beforehand I was thinking about what I'd say to my former friend when I saw him, but now that he's here, sitting at my table in uniform, I hold my tongue.

He tells us how on Trebević they mowed down the 'jihad' supporters like ripe corn with their machine-guns. Some of them had set out bare-handed and would get hold of a weapon only when one of their side died.

He says that his own brother called him up from Sarajevo, complaining that Serb soldiers had looted his flat. 'If I knew the co-ordinates, I'd shell that flat with my own hands. Doesn't he realize we're at war?', he fumes.

Unbelievable. His best friends in Pale were Muslims, he went to school and worked in Sarajevo, and now nothing emanates from him but hatred for those people and that city, even for his own brother, who's looking after his flat in Sarajevo.

He tells me: 'They wanted to search your house and take you away, but I saved you.' I reply that a few days ago eight soldiers did make a search, so I'm not sure how he saved me.

He's now a totally new and different man, though over the past year I've seen him simply abandon himself to an exclusively Serb national mythology. He'd be a ripe subject for a special analysis of how a man, an individual, who once thought at least partly with his own head, could so quickly drown in – and accommodate to –

this new wave of Fascist consciousness. Unless this has already been done by Danilo Kiš in his *The Anatomy Lesson*. That book is actually on my table, but next to it is one by Branimir Šćepanović which M.R considers conclusive evidence that we read Serb writers. I forebear to say that the book is there for 'The Goulash of Mr Goluža'.[15] My brain has stopped, and all writing about and description of human misery becomes superfluous.

Every rational remark I make, expressed with the maximum caution, bounces off him as if from an impermeable lump of stone. He now passionately desires what all Serbs must desire: to destroy the 'Turks' and their jihad, and to restore Serbia to its former glory and power. What would he say if he knew that my son was in Sarajevo, and that his shells from Trebević were falling also on him? (We've told everyone that the children are in England.) I tell myself: 'Be sensible, you have to survive and one day tell this man at your table the truth.' Is this cowardice on my part or good sense? If I tell him everything now, I'm done for.

His wife S. has gone over with astonishing speed from last year's 'disgust at those primitives from Pale' to a total submersion in and acceptance of their world and their way of thinking. She has become a greater Pale woman than the people from Pale themselves.

Our mutual friend, a comedian on Radio-Sarajevo, remains a riddle to me. He came with them, yet even the little he said doesn't fit into their framework. He says that his house on Osmice has burned to the ground, with a couple of thousand

---

15.   The well known story by Šćepanović is in fact 'The Death of Mr Goluža'. Vuksanović gives the wrong title here with sarcastic intent, in allusion to the author's participation in the Serb nationalist witch-hunt launched against Kiš following publication of his *Tomb for Boris Davidovich*, a witch-hunt to which Kiš himself responded precisely with *The Anatomy Lesson*, which includes a chapter titled 'The Double Goulash of Branimir Šćepanović'.[With thanks to Ivan Lovrenović.]

books. He can't blame anyone, since it was burned down by 'my Serbs – who made a mistake, so they say'.

I feel sorry for him, he's basically a good man, far better than these two sitting at our table this evening.

As they leave, M.R. forces upon me a whole stick of cigarettes, as if he can buy me with it – or wash clean his bloody hands.

My wife and I are left alone, and she keeps repeating: ' Why didn't I tell them this, why not that, why?' If it's a sin to be sensible and save one's life, then we're great sinners. We can be condemned by any Tom, Dick or Harry. We're nothing.

I listen to the midnight news. The first rays of hope seem to be breaking through: under international pressure, the Serbs have to withdraw from the airport and stop shelling Sarajevo.

I think of ways, as soon as my son leaves Sarajevo, to free myself from the deadly embrace of this freedom in Pale.

One hour after midnight. I feel calm and full of hope for tomorrow.

Pale, Saturday 27 June 1992

I go to the little shop near my house, owned by Enisa Musa, where I've being buying goods on credit on the understanding that I'll pay her once I have money. The shelves are completely bare. She tells me she can no longer get goods from anywhere: they simply won't supply Muslims. A few days ago a drunken Serb reservist, a chetnik, burst into her shop and put his pistol to her breast, threatening to kill her. She asks me where she can go, whom she can complain to? She's afraid for her husband and children. Pale is ruled by lawlessness and terror. She's still not thinking of leaving, but...

Refugees arrive daily enquiring about Muslim houses, or Muslims who might exchange their house for 'an even better one in the city'.

By a major effort of mind and will, I listen to the leader Karadžić saying on television how: 'America and Europe cannot grasp our reasons for bombarding Sarajevo and seizing the airport.' That man! Not a shred of pity or shame for what he has done to Bosnia in this short period of time that he has been in power.

The Serb news presenter Risto Đogo, my former colleague from Sarajevo TV's Channel 3, a great fan of the communists and Ante Marković, now says at the end of the news: 'That was the *second* news of the day' – while simultaneously holding up *three* fingers [Serb nationalist salute].

Perhaps in such poltroons lies the germ of the future collapse of the new regime. Like dogs, they're forever sniffing round in search of new masters who'll throw them fresh bones to gnaw.

Don't insult my animals!

Today I lent 100 German marks to a desperate pensioner, so that she could send her children and grandchildren to Belgrade, then on into the wide world. She thanks me tearfully, then my wife realizes that the woman is actually her old French teacher. 'What a small world', she says and thanks us again.

Pale, Sunday 28 June 1992

Save your honour first, then your life, I tell myself. I'm trying to get some medicines from Belgrade or Titograd for the gravely ill son of our neighbour Miralem. Poor man. He has a mentally ill son at home, and when he goes out he sees mentally ill and insane neighbours. He telephones from our house, then endlessly thanks us for the favour. His second, younger, healthy son has been sacked, while he no longer gets his pension, I don't know how they manage to live at all.

Fresh bombardment today of the entire city. As though they want to show their full power before withdrawing from the airport. My wife tells me with tears in her eyes that Đulzida has come to ask her to make a pair of her *dimije* into a skirt.

Midnight. News. Mitterrand and Bernard Kouchner are coming to Sarajevo. I met Kouchner in Dubrovnik in January '92, when he saved it from further destruction. Will he save Sarajevo? I'd give the man the Nobel Peace Prize.

On our table, in Mitterrand's honour, the biggest flower display ever.

Today at about ten o'clock in the graveyard I once again feel the stare of two bearded fellows with submachine-guns. All they can do to me is snuff me out as a human being. Not to go to the graveyard for fear of my life would be a total capitulation. I'd behave in the same way at my father's grave if the opposite lot of nationalists were in power here.

In the afternoon I have a long telephone conversation with my son in Sarajevo. He's proud of me and I of him. He has no money problems. My friends are taking care of him.

He tells me he saw his teacher Radoje on the Serb television news, shelling the city from Trebević.

A teacher killing his pupils. All values have collapsed.

Mitterrand and Kouchner walk through the streets of Sarajevo and lay flowers where those innocent civilians were killed in Vaso Miskin street.

Night. Euphoria in Sarajevo. The airport reopened and available for humanitarian aid. Perhaps Sarajevo's on the road to salvation, but for Bosnia it's a terribly long way off.

The time of thrashing about between life and death goes on. How can I get my son out of Sarajevo, and us out of Pale? What shall I do?

Pale, Monday 29 June 1992

I feel ice cold. Only now do I fully understand those desperate people who lost their lives trying to cross the Berlin Wall. Is there any point now in trying Honecker, when his victims are already forgotten? Or are they not forgotten, and must there be a trial?

Here I'm surrounded not by a concrete wall, but by a wall of sinister armed men who shoot at any human being who's not like them.

Today at last the UN flag fluttered over Sarajevo Airport.

I finished the wooden fence. My wife is in the garden watering flowers – yellow lilies. Luckily the 'clodhoppers', as my daughter calls them, aren't interested in flowers.[16]

---

16.   The term is *papci* , literally meaning 'cattle hooves'.

Pale, Tuesday 30 June 1992

4.30

Dawn is about to break. I'm happy not to hear the familiar sound from the direction of the city, and calm because the first aircraft carrying equipment for the UN forces landed last night.

No electricity, no telephone, but I see and hear within me the people I love.

The chirping of birds can be heard in the garden. The poison of hatred has diminished within me. I want only to help these unfortunate people around me. Already at eight o'clock on the bridge near my house a group of Muslim citizens gathers to wait once again for transport to Sarajevo. I talk to them. They explain to me that they've lost everything, all they have left is life itself, and it's better for them to go to Sarajevo than to wait in Pale for the executioner to arrive at their door. And even if they didn't have to leave, what would they live off, when they've all lost their jobs.

As they stand on the bridge, a family of Serb refugees from Vraca near Sarajevo is moving into my late mother's house.

What an absurd nonsense of a policy, violating life and its natural course.

I've no idea what's happening in Sarajevo. If I stay alive, the first thing I'll buy is an ordinary little transistor radio.

As noon draws near, my despair grows uncontrollably. Four hundred Serb families have been ordered by their leaders to leave Zenica and come to Pale; the same number of Muslim families must today or tomorrow leave all that they've built up here over the years.

As if people were pots of flowers. Even when we move flowers from one end of a room to the other, we take care that they don't wither and that they have enough light for survival.

What monstrous brain has thought all this up and is carrying it out? I know. The brain of war criminals, who must sooner or later be brought to trial.

A convoy of buses has already formed above the bridge. Men and women run towards it, carrying their bundles and dragging their weeping children. I hear wailing and lamentation.

Mina and her family are leaving too. Her daughter tearfully implores my wife to look after her dog Arči. She's no longer talking about 'needless panic'. They bring us two litres of oil and a bottle of spirits, even though we told them before not to bring us anything. My wife is in tears, she begs them not to go. 'If you go, I know we'll have to as well', she says.

As if I were dreaming the most terrible dream. I can see it all with my own eyes, but I can't believe it's true. I can't watch this nightmare. I hold back my tears.

Our neighbour Meho still hasn't left. He comes to me under the apple tree, and says nothing. My good friend from childhood Dado Musa, the maths teacher, hasn't left either; he comes to see us late in the afternoon and says he won't go till they put a knife to his throat.

He comes from one of the most eminent and oldest Pale families, a decent man who has never done harm to anyone.

I tell him not to go. They're just worried about their two young children. What might happen to them?

I hear about an appalling event: Izo, a barber from the *čaršija*, was taken to prison. The next day they told his family that he'd committed suicide by hanging himself. When they were preparing him for burial, they found numerous serious injuries on his body. He'd been beaten to death. Hardly anyone attended the funeral, out of fear.

How many people have perished like that in the Pale prison, no one knows. For many, entering its portals has meant only death.

Pale, Wednesday 1 July 1992

The exodus of Muslims continues in Pale. Like a snowball rolling downhill and growing bigger and bigger, the Muslims fleeing Pale are growing more and more numerous.

Something happened in their minds, something snapped and collapsed: the realization came over them that every hope they'd still cherished of surviving on their native soil had been definitively extinguished. Serbs with or without weapons circle their houses like vultures, taking their pick, certain that the Muslims *must* leave.

An exhausted Serb woman comes to our garden in tears. She says that she and her son moved into a little house on the slopes of Romanija. She's hiding her son so that he won't be called up, and is looking for somewhere in Pale for the rest of her family to live. She can't break into someone else's property, she'd feel too ashamed. She has asked some Serbs to take her into their already 'exchanged' large houses, where there's enough room, but nobody will even look at her, let alone help. She eyes our large house, and I tell her it's 'already reserved'. The woman can't stop weeping and cursing life, fate, politics.

In the surrounding hills towards Romanija, the Muslims are abandoning extensive farms, houses, cows, sheep, everything and – bundle in hand – making their way on foot to Pale, where already packed buses await them. Soldiers rummage through their belongings, to make sure they're taking nothing of value with them.

Neighbours tell me that every night there's shooting at houses which haven't yet been vacated. 'By fair means or foul' is the message.

'Decent Serbs' are horrified by this – but just that and no more. I reflect upon myself and my abhorrence, but how to oppose this wave that carries all before it? I know I'll be haunted till the end of my days by these images, and by the question: 'Couldn't I have done more?'

The restaurant owner Fadil, his eyes red from lack of sleep, comes into the yard bringing a bottle of cognac. He sits at the table and chain-smokes. He says that he invested all he had in the *Stari Most* [Old Bridge] restaurant, and is now losing everything. He has made some kind of 'deal' with three local Serbs, who will take it over it and 'run it till he gets back'. He smiles bitterly, tossing off his glass of spirits, and says that one day he really will be back.

He leaves, then the girls from Vučja Luka arrive. The telephone has just started working again, but they can't get through to their boyfriends in Sarajevo. As if all the phone numbers have been changed. The girls implore me, if I find some way of getting ourselves out, to find one for them too. They keep saying they'll go crazy. People with children are still running down the road towards the parked buses.

Miralem's son is pushing a trolley with two sacks of flour, with the aim of returning them to the nearby shop and getting at least a little money for their life in Sarajevo. S.M., an acquaintance from Ilidža, comes to see us, a university lecturer with a PhD who transferred to Pale to live in his sister's weekend cottage, and who complains that FAMOS (motor repairs) in Koran won't employ him, because they 'don't need him'. They need the occasional worker and lots of warriors. He sees only his own troubles, and is blind to the nightmare all round him.

Our marriage witness M. comes round bringing milk. She's crying, and says that all her dear, close neighbours are leaving their houses. How is she going to live now, with whom will she spend time? One of her sons, a doctor, fled to America two months ago; the other, a lawyer, left for Serbia and Montenegro ten days ago with his wife and children, abandoning his job at the municipality and with no intention of coming back. She can't comprehend what's happening around her. She stares at us with eyes wide open, a cup of tea trembling in her hand, and says: 'You won't be going too, will you? But *you* don't have to go!'

Completely unexpectedly, one of our best friends from Sarajevo, J.O., arrives at our house. He spent more than a month in Grbavica, hiding to avoid being called up. Since he's a valued specialist for the electric power system in B-H, he obtained from the Serb authorities installed at Hotel Bistrica on Jahorina a pass saying that they needed him, which enabled him to leave Grbavica and get through to our house in Pale. He has no intention of going to Jahorina, because his mother has remained in the Centar neighbourhood of Sarajevo, so he's afraid they might do something to her if they learned he'd gone across to the Serb side. He's hoping to 'dodge both sides' and escape to his wife's place in Belgrade. He'll now hide out at our place until he gets a permit to go to Belgrade. We're happy to hear from him that S.S. too is alive. Beaten, maltreated, but still released to go home and alive.

Night has fallen over Pale. I find it odd to see so many lit windows. A group of people is herding a large flock of sheep and ten cows with calves down the street. We can hear mooing and the barking of dogs. These are animals stolen from Muslim farms, on their way to the slaughterhouse or someone's shed.

My neighbour and childhood friend L. (forgotten the surname) walks up and down through the upper town with a submachine-gun at the ready, 'making sure nothing happens to the Muslims'. I think of how, in creating human beings, God must have vented all his anger. Out of pity he added the occasional spark of warmth, love and happiness, but such sparks were extinguished long ago in Pale.

'Each man has his own cross to bear', says Jesus before they crucify him on Golgotha. Each of us will one day have to render account to himself, but some to a war crimes tribunal.

We're no longer alone in the house. Our friend listens obsessively to every TV and radio station, in order to be as well informed as possible, which is of vital importance for his next moves.

He tells me the situation is unfolding to my advantage, because the Serbs and the Croats have reached an agreement to share power and divide up the territory. I look at him wanly and can't understand what he means. He's all rationality and calculation, and that kind usually survive. He even has a transistor.

Is it really July already? And I thought it would be all over back in May.

I'm beginning to panic. My son still hasn't received by fax from Rijeka the indispensable document that will allow him to leave Sarajevo on a Jewish convoy. I'd never have dreamed that his life would depend on his place of birth.

I think of a dear poet [Miloš Crnjanski] and his lines: 'The silence will come when all this fades away, and me, and me...'

Until late at night J. tells us about the Serb soldiers' reign of terror in Grbavica. People would have given all they had, just to cross over from that ghetto to the Sarajevo ghetto.

I note down how the 'beloved, courageous, etc' commander Z. died, whose funeral was shown on SRNA, saying that he'd been killed 'courageously and selflessly fighting for lofty Serb goals', and who'd announced a day earlier on camera that they'd captured Šoping by 'simply walking in'. He ignored an order that the Serb fighters should put on gas masks to distinguish themselves from their foes wearing identical uniform, so his own comrades shot him down.

Pale, Thursday 2 July 1992

Morning. Some uniformed men and some women and children are standing outside Meho's house. They're explaining something to him. Meho comes over to my house, and with trembling hands places a sheet of paper on the table – a contract temporarily ceding his house, his garden and his joinery tools to a Serb family. He begs me to sign it as a witness. I know that this piece of paper and my signature on it mean absolutely nothing. I'm ashamed to look him in the eye. This is the definitive departure of a neighbour and a friend, who'd woven his entire life into building his house and helping his children.

Another neighbour, R. Memija, implores me tearfully to let him store his freezer, stove and garden tools in my woodshed. In vain I explain to him that we too will be leaving soon. He doesn't listen to me, just weeps and brings some blankets and books for my wife to look after. A Serb family is already waiting outside the door of his modest flat.

I'm in despair, I'll go crazy witnessing these scenes.

Dado arrives to ask if he and his family can come over and sleep at our place tonight. He's afraid they'll all be massacred. He didn't want to leave, but a little while ago two armed Serbs (one was a pupil of his) held a submachine-gun to his throat and told him he had till tomorrow to get out of his house.

I go to the boiler room, from which it's impossible to see anything. But I can hear people's voices, children calling out, and the sound of the convoy of buses leaving Pale.

M. arrives, quite distraught, and tells us what's going on round her house. In her empty rooms and her attic she has stored quantities of technical equipment and tools that her Muslim neighbours have left for her to look after until they return.

She says:'Are they really going to return?'

I know nothing any more. I only know that even in my dreams I never imagined this happening in Pale. It's a crime, a terrible crime towards these poor people. I'm no longer at all concerned for myself. All this pain of others who are nevertheless close to me fills me totally and threatens to destroy me.

My wife looks at the bottle of spirits that Meho brought over before leaving and begins to weep. She says : 'Now it's our turn.' I know.

Only one thought goes through my head – this is not possible.

I go out into the garden and lie down on the bench under the apple tree. Strangers walk in and out of the nearby houses. They wander round surveying their booty. In Meho's garden and in Miralem's, vegetables flourish, wood is neatly cut and stored for .

winter. Where will they spend it now? They won't survive this, I tell myself.

Remember: 2 July 1992.

The sound of vacuum cleaners now reaches me from their houses. They're taking the bedding out to air, and making a pile of old things. For yesterday's tenants, those old things were treasured mementos of their parents, their childhood. Pale now looks like a mausoleum in which fresh corpses have been deposited.

I dial the number for the Television and ask if that's Sarajevo TV, and a rough male voice says:
'Whaddya mean Sarajevo? – This is Belgrade, mate!'

We realize that we're now connected directly to the Belgrade telephone system. How am I going to get through to Sarajevo now? Is there some area code, because we're getting Belgrade numbers without the 011 code? I realize too how in wartime a person depends utterly on the whim of some maniac or obedient executor of orders 'from above'.

The comedian M.J. arrives, a tragic figure of this war. He says he's trying to form a peace movement among Serbs in Pale. That would be like planting roses in the Siberian ice. He describes his attempts to get some prisoners released from the Lukavica and Kula prisons. He left his wife in Sarajevo, came to Pale and thus definitively crossed the demarcation line. There's no way back for him, while here he looks like Don Quixote. The only thing left to him is his 'dream of building masonry foundations in Slovenia, where he has many friends'.

It's evening. Dado arrived for the night with his wife and his two little boys. He brought a bottle of whisky along too. He says he has been keeping it for a 'special occasion'. As we sit at the table, the children never take their eyes off me. Do they understand what's going on? Dado and his wife force themselves to laugh, saying that all they care about is saving their children's lives.

Banging at the door. A tall young man in uniform, and a local Muslim from Pale who has been cooperating with the Serb authorities, ask whether Dado is there. I feel my bones turn to icy fear.

'We know he's here. You're the only person he could come to', they say and come into the main room.

'I told you I wouldn't do anything to you if you left tomorrow. You could have slept in your own home, I'd have taken care of you', the tall security policeman tells Dado.

As long as I live I shan't forget the look in those children's eyes fixed on me. They understood everything.

After my father's and my mother's death, this has been the most terrible day of my life. A dreadful punishment and plague has fallen upon us.

The uninvited guests leave, Dado goes with his wife and children to the upstairs bedroom to sleep, we go to our bedroom. I know he won't sleep a wink tonight, and nor will I.

J. listens through earphones to the news from the transistor.

I wait for dawn to break.

Pale, Friday 3 July 1992

At dawn Dado and his family leave. I don't know whether I'll ever see him again. We've spent together our entire childhood, our youth and our adult lives. Now a sinister, criminal hand that knows no mercy severs us like wood for kindling. I learn that the Serb authorities have taken a decision that all Muslims must leave Pale and the surrounding villages by 5 July.

A convoy of buses stands for hours on the main road. Same scenes as yesterday. More people come to ask: 'Are there any Muslim houses round here?' My wife says to one fellow, raising her voice: 'No, there aren't! Neither Muslim nor Croat ones! There were only *human* houses here.'

I've no strength left to go and say goodbye once again to Dado and other people I know. I've no strength left for anything, except despair.

'A crime begins with spiritual self-mutilation', writes Franz Kafka. Such truth in those words. Before this crime, the Serbs mutilated themselves spiritually.

I hide my diary even from our friend and guest J.O.

Pale, Saturday 4 July 1992

Everything's the same. The houses, gardens, roads, alleys, birds, flowers, only the people are totally different. All the friendly faces that for years I'd meet, see and greet each morning have now disappeared. Instead of them, the sinister, unfamiliar faces of strangers look at me.

As if some giant broom had simply swept away the old inhabitants and swept new people into the area.

An armed man in uniform with an eye missing comes into our yard and asks me whether I'd exchange the house for one in Pofalići (Sarajevo). In normal times that might even be a normal question, but in these times it's a clear sign that we're on the list of those who have to leave.

Late at night the phone rings. My wife answers and a voice says: 'You're still here?'

Another nocturnal visit from the Serb Television producer, who this time is sober. He assures us that, having been extreme, he has now become a 'moderate Serb'. He tells me that my High Commission for Refugees pass means absolutely nothing to the military authorities. Only if, on the basis of that, I get a permit from the *Dobrotvor* [Benefactor] association can I leave Pale for Belgrade. To Sarajevo I can go only in a coffin. He says he'll talk to the people at *Dobrotvor* about the permit. I'm grateful to him.

My friend J.O. hides in his room.

Pale, Sunday 5 July 1992

An early morning visit to the graves of my mother and my father. If they were alive, how would they survive this present nightmare in Pale? In 1944, when my father was taken from the house, his life was saved by a Muslim. We never forgot that.

The war began on this very day three months ago.

A ray of hope for my son's departure from Sarajevo.

My wife looks at the garden and says: 'It has never been more beautiful.'

I learn that a Croat 'Herzeg-Bosna' has been formed. The Serbs are triumphant, saying they'll easily come to an agreement with the Croats. They'll leave the scraps for the Muslims.

We can get Sarajevo numbers if we dial 071. They can't call us.

A friend from TV Sarajevo lets me know that he'll stop working tomorrow, since he can't put up with certain things that are happening there. Which things? What's going on at the Television centre?

A last convoy takes the remaining Muslims from Pale off towards the city. Among them is the restaurant owner Fadil, who has bought a whole sackful of sausages and other processed meats. He's afraid of hunger in Sarajevo. Some uniformed men are removing everything from his flat and loading it onto a lorry.

I didn't sleep all night. I drank Dado's whisky and, in a zombie-like condition, thought about boarding with my wife the bus taking the Muslims to Sarajevo. I just thought about it, but didn't actually do it, since that would have been pure suicide.

All we have now is alcohol in abundance. We get slowly drunk and wait. For what?

Pale, Monday 6 July 1992

Every move I make, every word I speak on the telephone, every conversation, can cost us our lives.

Good news fills me with hope that we and our son will somehow stay alive, but then an avalanche of bad news crushes it.

A heavy pall of smoke from burning Muslim belongings spreads across Pale and my garden.

I lie in bed and through the closed shutters listen to voices from Meho's house: 'Let's go and have coffee at the weekend cottage.' 'No, it's raining, let's stay at home.'

How many Serbs are there who, in addition to a house, have 'captured' a weekend cottage as well? Or several houses? To some people war is truly a friend. I remember how old people used to say that hungry eyes are never satisfied.

If these people think they'll find happiness and peace in other people's houses, then they're dreadfully mistaken. I'm convinced that one day the Serb people will live to see terrible moments. So many Muslims killed and driven out can never be forgotten.

Out of all the Muslims in the upper town, only Munira is left, whose husband was a Serb (her two sons are in Belgrade), and one old woman who wants to die in Pale. Just like the plague, I tell myself.

A self-employed electrician Đ.K., who before doing this job used to work at the Valter Perić power station, will move into our house with his family. He seems a decent person. He shows me how there are more Muslim numbers than Serb ones written down in his telephone book. Everything has become utterly absurd. My wife is glad that they have two sons who love animals, so when we leave, if we leave, and we must leave, they'll look after our two little dogs and our cat.

'Don't cry', I tell her, 'everything will be all right', but I feel like crying too.

Our friend listens non-stop to the news, and through some of his connections is trying to get a permit from the military authorities to leave for Belgrade.

Pale, Tuesday 7 July 1992

The 'grunting' of the guns can be heard all night again from the direction of Trebević. A person grows accustomed to everything, becomes inured, and finds it strange when all is quiet. There's no electricity either – heaven knows how many days it has been.

I'm engulfed in total apathy and hopelessness. I don't care if I get out of Pale alive or not. Life means nothing here.

News of the day on Serb TV: Dr Kecmanović, one of the Serb representatives on the B-H Presidency, fled from Sarajevo to Pale and then in a military helicopter flew on to Belgrade. Just what you'd have expected of that politician for all seasons. The Serbs are exultant.

The helicopters still have fuel. Our garden is becoming overgrown with weeds.

If we don't leave Pale soon, we'll be either dead or living alcoholics. We get quietly drunk every day on the spirits we got from our former neighbours. The smoke from the burnt Muslim belongings creeps into the house and I feel as though in Auschwitz.

Via London, Rome, Koper, Trieste, we try to sort things out regarding our son's document, which still refuses to arrive at the Jewish Community by fax from Rijeka.

Despair is overpowered only by our desire to save ourselves from this hell.

Pale, Wednesday 8 July 1992

Our three big travelling bags have already been taken out of the cupboard. They're still empty. I'm waiting for the permit from *Dobrotvor*.

I go out into the garden and sense the glances of our new neighbours, who stare at me oddly as if wondering what we're still doing here. They're the glances of the new masters of these parts, people who have moved into other people's houses as if it were the most normal thing in the world.

I hear that some of them have already come to blows over the boundaries of the land they've appropriated, over cows and over cars.

News of the day: Izetbegović is travelling to Helsinki, where Bush will receive him. Is this a step towards peace, or a leap into some yet deeper abyss?

In the evening, with my wife, I cross the road and go to visit our old family friends. They have two cows and that is their salvation. All their Muslim neighbours have left. They tell us about the horrors they've seen. Mrs Munira is there too, she has been sleeping at their place for days. A desperate woman, who doesn't know what to do, where to go. Our world has totally collapsed and now we're foreigners in this new one that's just being created. I wouldn't like either to live or to die in it.

Pale, Thursday 9 July 1992

'Then the sun came out and went down...', Samuel Beckett writes in his novel *Molloy*.

Here, in Pale, the sun no longer comes out at all. I finally got the permit from *Dobrotvor*. Apart from the two graves, my mother's and my father's, nothing in Pale matters to me any longer, neither the house nor the garden, absolutely nothing. Oh, yes. These two dogs. What will happen to them?

I say we'll leave on Tuesday, but I know even today may be too late.

Our family friend M.'s son, who fled to Montenegro, has returned and cannot cope here at all. He has been sacked from his job. If he wants them to employ him again, he has to volunteer for Trebević. He has to prove that he's 'a patriot, and not a traitor to his people'. He says he'd rather die than do that. But what will he live off?

He brought me a small parcel of food from my sister in Titograd. He says she just cries all the time.

Our son still hasn't received his documents. I'm panicking.

Pale, Friday 10 July 1999
A friend from Pale came to see me yesterday and quite calmly says he'll get a permit from the military authorities for my friend J.O. to leave with us for Belgrade on Tuesday. An honest and decent man, whom I can trust. Nevertheless we stare at him dumb-founded.

Today I have to go to *Dobrotvor* in person, a voice informs me over the phone. But how? I have to go down the main road, right through town, past the police station, the prison, the SRNA and Serb TV buildings. I have in my hands the document from the High Commission for Refugees as some kind of protection.

As I ride my bicycle down the street, I feel eyes watching me and feel my legs trembling. It's enough for one of them to shout: 'Hey, you, come here', and all is perhaps over.

I repeat to myself my mother's words, that God protects those who believe in Him. I'm received by a quite civilized fellow, who limits himself to saying they support all UN humanitarian activities.

As I ride back, my nerves are at snapping point.

I go to a nearby field to help our friends gather the hay. I go past Dado's house, and see how the furniture, carpets and rugs have all been carried out and are being washed with a hose. They've taken his car out of the garage and are inspecting it. When I go past again two hours later, the tenants are sitting under Dado's plum tree drinking *rakija*. Tears come to my eyes.

'I'll never go past here again', I tell myself.

Last night on TV I watch Vojislav Šešelj (dubbed the 'war leader', I remind myself)[17] coming out of the Assembly, brandishing a pistol and swearing at students who are chanting: 'Murderer, murderer, fag, fag!'

We should leave Pale on Tuesday. I can be dead a hundred times before Tuesday.

I can't go out into the garden because of Auschwitz.

I learn that one Muslim gave a cow to his neighbour, a local Serb, before he left. The Serb who moved into his house turns up with a pistol and leads off the cow, since 'she too goes with the house he got'.

My wife places an advertisement on the local Serb radio, saying that she has some terrier pups to give away. Soon a rough male voice calls up to ask what sort of houses (!) we're giving away.[18]

---

17.   Šešelj awarded himself the chetnik title of *vojvoda* or war leader.
18.   Untranslatable linguistic error arising from the near homonyms *kučiče* = pups;. *kučice* = houses (dim.)

Children of new Pale residents take the puppies away. What sort of destiny awaits those children and those dogs?

I look through the window at the green garden and slowly take my leave of it. My mother's parents dug it and laid it out, my mother cultivated it and planted it with vegetables throughout her whole life, we have tended it for some ten years and now it's the end. Perhaps I'll never see it again. The only thing I regret is not being able to send its produce to my friends in Sarajevo.

Pale, Saturday 11 July 1992

Mass death has descended on Goražde like a hurricane. One hundred thousand people are trapped in a cage. The forest creatures are systematically wiping them out.

Another visit from the drunken producer, who keeps toying with his pistol. He looks at me with bleary eyes and says: 'You won't be back! You're running away from Pale after all.' I explain to him once again that I'm not running away, that I've abandoned journalism for good, that my only concern now is humanitarian aid for wretched people of all nations, colours, races. Our friend J.O., who has always kept out of sight of all our visitors, suddenly comes into the room with earphones on his ears and the transistor in his hands. I see his face turn white as chalk. What carelessness. He didn't hear our voices because of the earphones. There's nothing I can say. I explain to the producer that he's someone who has just arrived from Grbavica, to work for the government of the Serb Republic of B-H. M.T. starts to provoke him, saying that he's no true Serb if he has only just now come to Pale, that his surname may even be an ustasha one, that...

Luckily, this highly dangerous questioning is interrupted by the arrival of the family who are moving into our house today.

The producer goes off, saying once again: 'You're leaving for good, whatever you say! A bullet in the head is the only thing in store for traitors.'

My wife reiterates that we'll go only when she finishes her weaving. We begin to consider what things we'll take with us. As if we're going on some business trip. I look at the house, the garden, my mother's house, and don't feel sad about anything. Life here is worse than death.

We make the acquaintance of the people who are moving into our house. We show them the rooms, tell them where everything is; I give them instructions on using the central heating, my wife on the kitchen equipment and the machines in her work room, and on how to look after the animals. We have lunch together. They lost their flat in Sarajevo, and we're now losing this house in Pale. Nothing terrible compared with the thousands of dead people all round us. This is only a momentary triumph of the monstrous policy of ethnically pure territories. I imagine – not so much imagine as already see – Pale as a Serb ghetto, and I say: 'I hope they bite and tear one another apart in this ghetto like hungry rats.'

Pale, Sunday 12 July 1992

Final visit to my father's and my mother's graves before our departure from this 'heart of darkness'. I say farewell to them. I feel they see me and understand. Everything is concentrated into one thought and desire – that our son should extricate himself from Sarajevo next week, and we from Pale.

I trust in God. No rational law is worth a thing here any more. A human being is like a straw borne by the storm wind.

My wife slowly packs our most essential belongings. What do we take? So many things, necessary or superfluous, collected in these twenty years of life together.

I assure her that now, if we get out of here alive, we'll begin a new cycle of life. Start again from nothing and get somewhere. Once I used to be terrified by Kafka's sentence: 'On other roads, there are other stations of hopelessness.' Once reason enough for suicide, now reason enough to live.

Pale exists for me only as the memory of the wonderful people with whom I spent my childhood and my youth, of meadows and forests, of snow and skiing, of drinking and loving. This Pale of today has for me been buried in a tomb and no longer exists.

If they don't let me leave here on Tuesday, I shan't despair, it will merely be life in the tomb, with the hope of one day escaping from it.

My wife is showing the new tenants what grows where in the garden. Then she goes off to weave.

The dogs lie beside my feet as if they sense an immiment parting. Those wonderful creatures that know nothing of evil, hatred or death.

We're happy to see the girls from Vučja Luka, who have come to telephone. We've become so fond of them that we've adopted them as our own children. Now we must part from them as well. I tell them I know, I feel, that we'll meet again some day.

I go to say farewell to N.K., the old friend of my parents. He says: 'If you go, who will bury me?'

Pale, Monday 13 July 1992

Oh God, what relief, what joy. I manage to get through via Trieste to my friend A.D. in Koper, who tells me that the document for my son has been sent by fax to Sarajevo and has been received. A huge weight off my mind.

I buy bus tickets for ourselves and J.O. He should get the permit tonight from my friend in Pale.

We can't believe that all this is real. As evening falls, my wife comes out of her work room and says: 'We can go now, I've finished my weaving.'

Darkness has fallen, but the friend isn't here yet with the permit. At about ten, as I wander distractedly round the house, the friend arrives bringing the permit, which he says he forgot about when he went with his mates to a bar. We laugh bitterly. To forget about a paper on which a life hangs.

Another weight off my mind.

I'm superstitious. The unlucky 13th is perhaps the luckiest day of my life. If only my son gets away too.

How can I sleep through this night, when I don't know what awaits us on the journey?

A desperately long night.

I'll go on writing when I get to Rijeka.

If I ever do.

Rijeka, 15 July 1992

I thank you, O Lord. We're here at last, in Rijeka.

In my thoughts I go back to the morning of 14 July, when we set out from Pale.

Our dear friend M. has come to see us off. Her eyes are red from weeping, her thin body even thinner. I go into the garage, and beside the figure of the Virgin Mary I place some money and implore her to help us on the journey. I give the garage key to M., assuring her that we're not leaving forever, that we'll be back in a month or two. I can see she doesn't believe me.

The first military checkpoint is at the bus station itself. They don't get us out of the bus. We can proceed.

We drive through Pale. If we can only leave! The second checkpoint is on Romanija, at Sokolac, the third near Han Pijesak, the fourth on the way in to Vlasenica ... the ninth on the Drina, near Zvornik – the former border between Serbia and Bosnia-Herzegovina. An assortment of people in uniform carry out the checks, with or without beards, with cockades and various other badges on their caps. They look respectfully at my identity card saying that I was born in Pale and live there. For them that is the best recommendation, since to be from Pale means to be among the first fighters for a free Serb republic.

I look from the bus at destroyed and burnt out houses, feeling as if I'm travelling through the underground world of Dante's Inferno.

In Zvornik we encounter a long convoy of white UNPROFOR trucks. I look at the youthful, relaxed faces of the drivers and their escorts, and wonder if they'll be like that on the way back. They've set off as if for a picnic, to experience a bit of excitement in Bosnia and earn some money, but they'll come back with indelible scars on face and mind. Some will die in the Bosnian inferno.

At about 14.00 we arrive in Belgrade. B.O. is there to welcome us with hugs and kisses, and when she eventually sees her husband too emerging from the bus, she utters a shriek of joy and surprise. We're all incredibly happy, they because they're together and in the place of their birth, we because we're so close to the Hungarian border.

At 21.00 we leave by bus for Hungary. Another weight falls from my mind when we pass through the Hungarian frontier. I'd like to get out and kiss the ground, like in a scene from some tear-jerker. A long journey by night through an unknown land, then at dawn we halt at the Slovenian frontier. Some Roma emerge from a bus and get into ours, while we cross over to theirs. A heavy odour of food remnants, unwashed bodies and tobacco.

Wednesday 7.00, Slovenian frontier, Murska Sobota – Dolga Vas

We've been waiting in the bus for over two hours already for them to let us across the frontier. Cattle trucks loaded up with calves stop alongside us. We stare at each other and I don't know where the difference lies.

One more checkpoint and we're at last in Slovenia. A huge billboard saying 'Clean *deẑela* '.[19]

People make business out of everything. *'Money is freedom'*, a close friend of mine told me long ago. We pay some private carrier in foreign currency for a ticket to Ljubljana, where we arrive at around noon.

---

19.   *Deẑela* is the Slovenian word for country, homeland.

I can't get accustomed to the new scenery so quickly. There are no ruined or burnt out houses, no men with guns questioning you. People are working round their homes in peaceful tranquillity. That's how Sarajevo and Bosnia looked only three months ago. The memory of Pale slowly fades into the darkness.

One more checkpoint. Šapjane – the Slovenian frontier with Croatia – a somewhat longer interrogation, on account of my place of birth. The policeman smiles as he puts a stamp in my passport. The *šahovnica* flutters over the border post.[20] I experience a flash of memory from Pale, where our former friend forbade his son to play chess because it reminded him of the *šahovnica*.

At 16.30 we arrive in Rijeka. We're here, and what now?

We've lost our jobs, our house and our land in Pale, our Muslim friends who are now in Sarajevo dodging shells and waiting for a crust of bread, and our Serb friends from Pale who have enough bread but eat it with bloody hands. But we haven't lost our honour, or our experience of a terrible war, or the desire to plant a sprig of parsley or a currant seedling on the red soil of Istria. 'The glass is broken, but you can still drink from it.'

---

20.   The traditional red-and-white chessboard or checkerboard that has figured on the Croatian flag or coat-of-arms since the middle ages.

So It Was Foreseeable

Afterword by
Roman Arens and Christiane Schlötzer-Scotland

In the days before Mladen Vuksanović began his diary on 5 April 1992, the Indian UN General Satish Nambiar was fitting out his headquarters in Sarajevo. Precisely on the same street that would sarcastically be labelled 'Sniper Alley' a few months later. The General had the task of supervising the unstable peace in the neighbourhood, in Croatia, from a formidable concrete barrack. His UNPROFOR soldiers still had the opportunity to roam through the picturesque old town in Baščaršija, casual as curious tourists in their pale blue berets. It was not yet necessary to put up the warning '*Pazi Snajper*' (Beware of Snipers) in all corners of the city.

During that time, however, fears and forebodings were beginning to emerge alongside growing tension and insecurity. When the glass roof of the concourse at Sarajevo airport broke during a storm and splinters exploded across the hall, a number of the travellers waiting for their flights threw themselves to the floor. Too late, they probably thought to themselves, the shooting has already begun. During the long hours of waiting in the cold airport, they could clearly observe extensive movements by the troops who were to later mount a siege and shell the helpless city from the skies.

Two thirds of those eligible to vote had expressed their support for the independence of Bosnia-Herzegovina, although the Serbs had demanded a boycott of the referendum. Barricades were erected at the beginning of March, after a violent incident at a wedding in the old Serbian Orthodox church in the city centre. Most of the tension, however, had dissipated during a nocturnal celebration, when thousands of Sarajevo's inhabitants who did not want to give way to the hysteria had overrun the barricades, and the military authorities were forced to retreat.

This operation led by peaceful citizens could not be repeated at the beginning of April 1992. When a large number of people assembled to demonstrate in front of the parliament and government buildings, with the intention of presenting a petition for prudent solutions, shots were fired from the Holiday Inn on the opposite side of the road. At this point, most hopes that the march towards war could still be stopped vanished.

The faint hopes were likewise soon gone that recognition of Bosnia-Herzegovina by the European Community on 6 April would still have the power to halt the warmongers. For the latter rightly realized that 'internationalization' of the conflict through such recognition was worth no more than a scrap of paper, and that the so-called world community would leave the newly recognized state pretty much alone in its fight for survival. 'A' had been said, but it was denied that 'B' must follow. Europe could not and would not unite on this 'B', so instead it preferred to participate in pompous rounds of negotiation at Geneva.

The war rapidly took more and more victims, and became more and more horrific. The army of the Bosnian Serbs expelled and killed countless people for the single reason that they considered themselves another ethnic group. 'Ethnic Cleansing' – one started to get used to this expression. The civilian population was inundated with acts of terror. Hundreds of thousands lost their homes and fled. All this already in the spring and summer of 1992, in the 110 days during which Mladen Vuksanović wrote his diary at his birthplace of Pale.

Isolated there, 'I was not able to witness or to register many incidents that took place in Pale'. But objectively restricted, fragmented observation there in that rather agreeable little place, which was not at all suited for the role of 'Republika Srpska' capital that had been forced upon it, allowed something to become disturbingly clear. Even more than from all the hectic, bewildered reports about shell and bomb attacks down in Sarajevo, it became apparent from the description of the changes in Pale that this war had not developed and expanded by chance, but according to a methodical procedure. Power interests were the aim, ethnically grounded hysteria was the motor leading to this aim.

Stupefying that everything was decided upon so early, but also that this could have been predicted. Mladen Vuksanović knew whither the war was leading in its first three months. There is an unbroken line from what happened to him and many others in Pale to massacres like the one in Srebrenica in July 1995. This sequence had its own dynamic, entirely different from that of the swift, bewildering alternation of peace conferences, peace plans and peace mediators. After which the war would each time renew and take unexpected turns that increased suffering immeasurably.

The shooting and bombardment could be halted only by military means and massive threats. This objective was contractually settled at Dayton, Ohio in November 1995. The solemn signing of the Dayton Agreement in Paris in the middle of December 1995 raised many hopes, although the preconditions for a stable peace were at that time still very distant, as they still are today. One condition for peace would be justice for the refugees – not just on paper. Mladen and Jadranka Vuksanović would have to be able to return to Pale and live there unmolested. But a person who had written this kind of a book about how everything began would be treated with hostility for a long time. Many people would not like at any cost to be confronted with what they did in the spring of 1992. Many no longer want to know exactly what happened, because it is difficult to bear.

This is the starting-point for the revisionists, who have long made their appearance on the scene with their obliging manipulations of this or that aspect of the truth. The Slovenian writer Drago Jančar encounters them: in the beginning, you would have known 'who is the victim and who the violent criminal; today you wonder: is what we saw on the television screens true, are the testimonies of the people who survived the siege of the unhappy city real, or are they instead the delusions of a sick imagination?'

The witness from Pale gives a clear answer to this – precise and verifiable. He has described three and a half decisive months in the spring of 1992, during his isolation.

The Witness from Pale

On 13 June 1992 Mladen Vuksanović writes the following in his diary: 'If these war criminals are ever brought to trial, I shall be a witness from Pale, this "heart of darkness".' In mortal danger, he notes how the ethnic cleansing machinery has spread from Pale to the whole of Bosnia in only a few weeks. He hides his diary even from friends, because the journalist and filmmaker does not know which of his colleagues of many years will betray him tomorrow. On 13 July 1992, Vuksanović adds his diary to the few pieces of luggage for his departure from Pale.

Three years later, in July 1995, he wishes to have his notes published, not wanting 'to die of shame for my silence' . There is still war in Bosnia. The refugee Vuksanović has found work in a youth detention hostel on the Croatian island of Cres. From there he writes a letter to the German-based *Journalisten helfen Journalisten* (Journalists Help Journalists – JhJ). He has obtained the Munich address from friends.

JhJ, founded in August 1992, is a solidarity organisation for dead, wounded and exiled colleagues and their families in the former Yugoslavia and other crisis areas. At the beginning of the war in Bosnia, journalists were still delivering donations directly from Germany, taking two hundred marks from their wallets, or buying sugar, cigarettes and coffee for the colleagues in need. Later JhJ concerned itself with other things that were necessary for survival – computers, medicines, operations, exit permits; money for accommodation, for school books, or for the daily routine as a refugee – in response to hundreds of letters.

Mladen Vuksanović asked JhJ for help with his daughter in 1995. He could arrange her flight to England, but lacked the means to support her everyday life there. In his letter he also mentioned his Pale diary. He wrote: 'I should like to know whether such a document on Karadžić's aggression, and on the genocide of the Muslims and other normal people, could be of interest to anyone.'

The explosive nature of these records from Pale remained hidden at first, because there was no translation of the text. This changed a few months later, after a chance encounter on the Adriatic island of Cres. During a stroll on a deserted beach, Vuksanović met a man previously unknown to him. The two men's dogs sniffed one another. Their owners then struck up a conversation. They both told each other about their friends in Germany, and soon realized they were speaking about the same friends.

The second man taking a stroll on the beach was the publisher Nenad Popović from Zagreb. He had been in contact for a long time with JhJ. At around the period of Vuksanović's isolation in Pale, Popović sent a letter to Germany. He addressed it to the German reporter Roman Arens, whom he had met before in Zagreb. In this letter Popović sought support for the family of a 29-year-old radio reporter Ivan Marsić from Croatia, killed by a bomb splinter. Popović's letter was – after the death of the German reporter Egon Scotland in July 1991 in Croatia – the catalyst for the foundation of JhJ.

By the end of that stroll on the island of Cres, Popović had the Pale diary in his hands. He was quick to recognize the quality of the document. It came out only a short while later, in 1996, from his publishing house Durieux in Zagreb, in the 'Ex ponto' series founded in 1995 with the support of the Swedish Helsinki Committee for Human Rights. Popović called Vuksanović's notes the 'chronology of an internal numbness', a 'belated epitaph for all those European cities whose inhabitants were scared out of their beds and driven from their doors in the grey light of dawn.'

Subsequently, the Germanist Popović had the task of recommending this diary to his friends in Germany. JhJ facilitated and supported the translation of the text, which was not merely an unusual document. Vuksanović's diary would ensure that, after the end of the war, history would not be hidden behind false legends. For journalists and authors were not on the side only of the victims during this war, there were criminals too among their number. Vuksanović describes this with ruthless openness. Hence, his diary should be a cautionary reminiscence for the future.

Journalisten helfen Journalisten